# Dedication

I dedicate this book to my husband who has been both
secretary and critic;
To my daughter and son who at an early age learned to
be quiet and good, so I could write;
And to my dear mother who inspired me to write it.

Nora Ann Kuehn.

# Contents

## Chapter 1

# The Day the Sun Stopped Shining

It was one of those days in early spring when everything is so breathtakingly beautiful, it would seem that nothing could go wrong. The gossamer tint of the sunrise was just wafting across the sky; a meadowlark gracefully soared into the air, cascading a musical scale skyward. My spirit lifted up, up with each lilting note.

My heart swelled with peace and happiness as I watched Tom, my husband, walk briskly across the alfalfa field to join Eric Johnson at the logging site.

Tom had big dreams of making extra money logging the majestic pines that grew straight and tall on forty acres of our section of land.

"We can pay off the mortgage, maybe even build a bedroom for Aaron," he had said when offered a price too good to refuse for the timber.

I picked a fading blossom from the soft blanket of yellow roses that tumbled over the back fence. We could certainly use that other bedroom. Aaron had outgrown the goldfish, frogs, and all the other things a seven-year-old brother like Darcy collected.

I was still picking off the faded roses when I saw Eric Johnson's truck bouncing up our lane. Eric was our friend and closest neighbor. I could tell there was something wrong by the way he was driving up the rutted road in total disregard of the many rocks and chuckholes. He didn't slow down until he brought the truck to a quivering stop beside the fence.

"Tom has been hurt!" he said as he jumped from the truck.

I stood frozen, mute with fear. Eric took my arm firmly, his face white and stern. "You can't fall apart, Kate; Tom needs you. We have to go to the hospital."

"Hospital!" I gasped.

Eric nodded. "Doctor Coltin couldn't do much for Tom at his office."

Aaron stepped out on the porch, rubbing the sleep from his eyes. He saw Eric and heard the fear in my voice.

"Where's Dad?" he asked, leaping down the steps.

"Your father is in the hospital," Eric said. "There was an accident in the woods."

I found my voice: "Aaron, you and Wanda will have to do the chores and look after Darcy. Eric is taking me to the hospital." I hugged Aaron to me for a moment; I could feel the fear in his tense young body.

"Dad will be all right, won't he?" His eyes pleaded with me for assurance.

"We will leave it in God's hands," I said, giving him another hug and hurrying to the truck.

I could hardly believe my eyes as I stood beside Tom's bed in the hospital. This wasn't the man who earlier that morning had been so filled with life and health. His face resembled gray paper, and his dark eyes were rolled back until they were colorless.

In a daze I signed the necessary papers and watched as Tom was wheeled into surgery. After the big swinging doors closed behind him, Eric led me back to the small waiting room. "I wish my mother were here," I said.

"I could go and get her, but I don't want to leave you here alone," Eric said thoughtfully.

"I'll be all right," I promised.

Assured that I would be fine, Eric went after Mother.

I picked up a magazine and, finding a quiet spot by the window, sat down to read. Two hours passed, and the magazine lay on my lap with the same picture on the front page still staring up at me. I turned to put the magazine back and saw the dear face that had always been there for me in times of need. My mother's arms stretched out to me, and I ran into them. She was holding me in her warm embrace when the doctor, still in surgical gown and cap, came to tell me that Tom had died in surgery.

My mind raced with silent questions to God as Eric drove us home. I saw the children at the door and wondered how I could ever tell them their father was gone. As I stepped up on the porch, Darcy flung his arms around my waist. I saw Mother look over at Aaron, who was holding onto the door like he might fall if he took his hand away.

"You and Wanda take Darcy upstairs," Mother told Aaron.

"We'll be up in a minute to talk to you."

Aaron scooped Darcy up in his arms, and Wanda followed, their slumped forms a study in grief.

"Oh, Mother," I sobbed, "how can I ever tell them?"

She patted and rubbed my heaving shoulders. "There won't be much more to tell," she said softly. "They've read all the answers in our faces."

I slumped down in the nearest chair and buried my face in my hands. "What am I going to do now?"

Eric, who had been twisting his hat in his suntanned hands and looking miserable, came over and put his arm around my shoulders. "I will come over and do any chore you or the children can't manage."

"You know I'll stay until you decide what you want to do about the farm," Mother said softly.

I went through the ordeal of the funeral like one in a trance. I was only too willing to let others take care of the arrangements that had to be made. It was my dear mother and Eric who stood by my side and handled everything for me. Eric took over all the farm work that the children and I couldn't handle. Friends and neighbors came to offer condolences and help. The weeks passed quickly.

Every morning, Wanda and Aaron caught the school bus at the end of the lane to go to the high school in town. Darcy was still attending the rural school about a mile from the farm. Tom used to take him to school on his way to work, but now Darcy was walking. When I worried about him, Mother insisted, "It's nice weather, and the walk won't hurt him. In bad weather I can take him in the car."

Darcy didn't seem to mind the walk through the woods to the schoolhouse. There was only one problem. No matter how early I started Darcy out for school, he always managed to be late.

One morning I wiped the steam-covered windowpane and watched as he scuffed across the yard, swinging his lunch pail. Surely, I worried, he would be on time *this* morning. Normally, a brisk walk would take anyone to the school house in twenty minutes. The hour I was giving him this morning should be more than enough.

My thoughts were still with him as I returned to bouncing the wooden dasher in the old crockery churn. Of course, Darcy was only seven, yet it wasn't too soon to think about molding his character. He was a good little fellow, but he had such a lackadaisical air about him. Start him on a chore, and it wasn't long before he would be involved with something else, completely forgetful of his first task.

It is sobering to realize that you will have to raise children alone. Their father had been such a hardworking man. "Salt of the earth," the neighbors had said, after he was gone. I was proud to hear my neighbors refer to my husband in that fashion, but what, I wondered, would Darcy's reputation be?

*Late to school . . . late to school . . . late to school,* the dasher in the old churn seemed to say. I thought of the note that Lester Clark, the schoolteacher, had sent home the previous evening with Darcy.

"It's important for students to arrive on time, Mrs. Gills," he had written. "Darcy has been tardy every day this week."

On sudden impulse, I removed my apron and ran across the yard, scattering lazy hens in my haste. Late every single day this week! Why, it was actually a disgrace! I would see to it that he got to school on time today. The shortcut to the country road went through the woods, and I walked carefully over the narrow, pine-needle-covered trail. I was mildly surprised at the mellow wood scent I'd forgotten in the past busy weeks.

I saw Darcy beside the creek, battered lunch pail at one side, wholly absorbed with something in the water. Exasperation rose in me. That explained why he was always late!

A footfall betrayed me, and he turned his round, snub-nosed face forward me. The shock of rust-brown hair was in his eyes again. He was an odd little miniature of his father.

"Ssh!" he said. "Look!'

There was movement in the underbrush across the creek, and a muskrat swam out to eye us curiously.

"Ho, you," Darcy called. "What'cha catch this morning?"

The small animal turned and leisurely coasted back to its hiding place on the opposite bank.

"I see him every day," Darcy explained, as if that ended the matter. "Sometimes I toss pebbles and he swims over and it's sort'a like a game. . . . " The glance he gave me was not entirely approving. "He's scared of you, though. I guess he doesn't like grown-ups."

"Doesn't he, though! Well, I think we'd better pick up our lunch pail, Darcy Gills, and get along to school!"

"Oh, school, well—s'long, Mom."

"I'll just go along a stretch, Young Man." The lecture I had planned didn't materialize. He looked so small and vulnerable.

He trudged along beside me, up and along the pine-scented path. It was pleasant in the woods, I was forced to admit, scarcely aware that I was walking more slowly.

Suddenly, I realized that my son was not beside me.

"Darcy! Darcy Gills!" I shouted. I walked back down the path and saw him squatting, his head low over the trail. I went over to see what he was watching with such intense interest. A few shiny black ants traveled up and down imperceptible highways, meeting, touching, and hurrying on again.

Darcy opened his lunch pail, crumbled a part of a sandwich for the ants, and absentmindedly munched the remainder.

"Got something else to show you, Mom," he said after a while. He went ahead of me to a clearing where a fallen pine had started its slow process of decay.

"Over here in these bushes, Mom!"

I caught my breath at the sight of the web, glistening in the morning sunlight, patterned with perfect delicacy.

"Now watch, Mom!" He tossed a rolled-up leaf into the web so that it hung, trembling slightly, on the silvery tracing.

I hardly breathed as I watched; a brown spider danced as though on a tightrope.

"He likes flies." Darcy's hand flashed in the air near the log. He brought it close to the web and released the insect.

"The spider eats flies, and frogs eat spiders, and snakes eat frogs," he explained soberly. "That's nat'chrul history, Mom."

"Yes," I said. "I suppose it is."

Tom came into my thoughts, and I recalled a summer day spent with him on a wooded hillside. I remembered the way his curly hair fell unheeded over one brown eye and his deep, thoughtful voice as he drew a small rectangle into the leaf-rich loam.

"If every man could have one acre of the Lord's good earth, there might be hope for peace in all the world."

There came the distant tolling of a bell.

Darcy gave a small cry. "Oh, Mom, the school bell!"

"Hurry," I cried, shoving the lunch pail at him. "Oh, Darling, run. You're going to be late again!"

I watched the small puffs of dust as his feet scampered to the country road and raced around the turn.

I walked slowly back and sat on the log. The spider was gone. The web was as it had been—silvery with dew.

"If every man owned a single acre of the Lord's good earth—" *Dear God,* I thought, *let Darcy grow up to be just the same.*

When Darcy returned from school that evening, Gram asked, "Did you make it to school on time today?"

"Barely," Darcy said, flashing me an elfish grin.

Gram led him to the old blackboard that hung over the kitchen counter. It was used for keeping records of the coming events around the farm.

The entry "Silly Biddy—Sept. 10," indicated that the bantam hen's eggs would hatch the tenth of September. Now, Gram wrote Darcy's name on the board. Then, taking a new piece of chalk from her apron pocket, she drew a star at the end of his name. She gave him a hug and said, "We will add a star for each day you are not tardy. The first week you get all stars, we will do something to celebrate."

"What'll we do?" Darcy asked, his eyes sparkling.

"Oh, I'll think of something you'll like," Gram said. "Maybe I'll take you to the sale barn with me some Thursday evening."

"Can I buy something?" Darcy asked.

"Maybe," Gram replied.

Other stars were added to the blackboard that fall— stars for hated chores done without complaining or a high mark on a report card—while I drifted and pondered how I was going to handle my own problems. I knew I had to decide whether to keep or to sell the farm. Still, day after day, I procrastinated.

## Chapter 2

# No Looking Back

Each new day I shifted to "automatic" and toiled at the endless chores around the farm. At night I fell into bed exhausted but couldn't sleep. I was overwhelmed and emotionally incapacitated with worry and sorrow.

Two months after Tom's death I decided my only hope of finding peace of mind was to sell the farm. I would start over in a place with no old ties or reminders of the past.

One morning I decided it was time to discuss my plans with Mother. We were at the round oak table by the kitchen window. It had always been my favorite spot in the old farmhouse. A light breeze ruffled the daisies bordering the path that led to the barn. Could it be that two short months ago my only worry had been to keep Darcy from battering the heads off the daisies with his lunch pail?

"You are looking gloomy this morning," Mother said, refilling our cups with more hot chocolate.

"Sorry it shows," I said wearily. "When I think of all the work Tom and I put into the farm, I can't help but feel bitter. This logging venture was to put us in the clear and fulfill some of our dreams."

Mother looked worried. "Kate, it's time to stop looking back," she said softly. "Remember, the Bible tells us that

14

no man who puts his hand to a plow and looks at things behind him is well fitted for the kingdom of God. To make a furrow straight, a plowman has to look ahead. Tom is gone, but you can carry on the goals you started together."

"I don't want to carry on. The sooner I can sell the farm, the better I'll like it."

"Then you have finally decided what you want to do?"

"Yes," I replied. "I have to get away from all these memories."

The sudden bang of the screen door caused me to look up in time to see Aaron's grief-stricken form streaking toward the old barn. He must have come downstairs just in time to hear me say I was selling the farm.

A worried frown creased Mother's brow. "I'm glad you have come to some decision, Kate. That boy needs to know there is still a hub for the family wheel. It's time to talk things over with the children and let them know where they stand too. All of you have just been drifting in limbo."

I put on my tattered chore coat and set leaden feet on the familiar path.

I knew it wasn't going to be easy to tell a boy who had already suffered the loss of a father that he must now give up the farm he loved.

Cindy, the Jersey cow we had raised from a bucket-fed calf, lowed softly in recognition as I entered the dilapidated barn. I knew the barn wouldn't be an asset to the sale of the farm, but I loved every rotten board on it.

I had milked my first cow in this old barn. All of the children had had their turn standing in the manger to watch me do chores while they were very small.

I thought of one morning when Aaron was four. He had bought a package of gum with some of his birthday dollar. I think he must have had the whole package in his mouth that morning, when an inquisitive cow nudged him with her nose while reaching for hay in the manger where he stood.

"Cow, you chew your own gum!" he yelled in fright, sure that the cow was trying to get his gum away from him.

Tom had laughed when I told him about it. After that, whenever we saw a cow peacefully chewing her cud, we would say, "She must have gotten Aaron's gum."

Every spot on the farm held a memory.

Under the sprawling willow tree was the spring where Wanda, with only her toes clinging to the casing, had hung inside to catch a frog. I had stood with heart hammering against my ribs, too afraid to yell at her for fear her small foothold would be lost and she would go tumbling head-first into the spring.

The silly lump was growing in my throat as I walked to the manger to gather the hay Cindy had nudged out of reach. With a proud cackle a speckled hen flew out of the manger. I took the egg from the nest and with it warm in my hand sat down on the slanting lid of the feed box.

I was fighting the lump in my throat when Aaron's arm encircled my shoulders.

For a long, agonizing moment there were no words, then Aaron said, "Mom, isn't a farm the nicest place in the whole world?"

I could only nod, remembering his father asking me the same question the day we decided to buy the farm.

Somehow, I knew in that instant that I could never sell our place. The children had lost their father, but they were not going to lose their home.

I thought I heard the word, "You will never be alone!" as I felt the heavy burden of sorrow lifting from my shoulders.

Mother and Darcy were in the kitchen. They stood in front of the blackboard, where Mother was adding another star beside Darcy's name. She looked up as I bounced into the room on feet that had left their shackles in a weathered old barn.

"You have decided to keep your home," she said as soon as I was inside the door.

"How did you know?" I stammered.

She gave me a wry grin. "Because I didn't raise a quit-ter."

She came over and gave me a hug. "Well, Partner, it

won't be easy, but if you will plow a straight furrow until we get these kids grown up, I'll give you a red star." She held up the piece of chalk with a chuckle.

"Did I hear you say, Partner?" I asked with renewed enthusiasm. "Would you really come and make your home with us?"

"Do you think I'd stay in a tiny apartment if I had a chance to live on a farm again?" she asked, her eyes shining with excitement.

"You have a chance," I said with a happy heart. "I'll plow a straight furrow too," I said sticking out my lower lip to look stubborn. "I'll earn that red star."

Mother laughed. "You always were the most determined and stubborn child I had."

A week later, Mother moved in to stay. She brought only two things from which she did not want to part—a rocking chair that had once belonged to my grandmother, and the old barrel cactus I remembered while growing up.

Now, Mother set the cactus in my kitchen window, the rocking chair in the chimney corner, and she was right at home. Like a mother hen, she gathered child and grandchildren under her comforting wing.

# Chapter 3

# Kid on the Roof !

Each of the children had his or her problems, but I was especially worried about Darcy. He was now getting to school on time, but he was too quiet and listless at home. His report cards and notes from his teacher showed his grades were failing.

After school, he would take his book of Bible stories and climb up into the treehouse his father had built for him in the orchard.

One afternoon I found him there. The book was open on his knees, but he wasn't reading. Tears were running down his tanned cheeks. With a grubby little hand he wiped away his tears, but he couldn't erase the sadness from his blue eyes.

It was soon after this that I noticed he had little appetite, and often what he did eat didn't stay down.

I took him to the doctor for a checkup.

"Just a nervous stomach," the doctor said. He gave me a prescription, but the medicine didn't help much.

One evening Mother came home from the livestock sale with a nanny goat and her kid riding in the back of the pickup. Soon we were having less trouble with Darcy's stomach. Nanny's milk seemed to be just what he needed.

18

Now Kid was our trouble.

Kid was all fun and games. She bounced around on her nimble feet like she had springs in all four legs. She climbed like a cat, jumped like an athlete, and ran like a deer. In spite of Kid's antics, everyone loved her except Miss Bell.

Miss Bell had been a thorn in our side ever since we bought the farm. She lived down the road from us in a big white house. Miss Bell was a spinster who had lived there alone as long as any of our neighbors could remember. She didn't like cats or dogs, and she had told us on one occasion that she didn't even like children.

On the day Kid got out of the orchard and nipped some of Miss Bell's rosebuds, she rattled up to our house in her old Ford, bringing one of her debudded rose branches. "Mrs. Lewis," she huffed, brandishing the rose branches like a sword at Mother, "those blasted goats have to go!"

Mother quietly guided Miss Bell to a seat on the porch swing and handed her a glass of lemonade. "I'm sorry about your roses, Miss Bell," Mother said softly. "I guess we will just have to keep Kid tethered; she is so inquisitive."

"Downright destructive!" Miss Bell sputtered.

"The goats are a bit destructive," Mother admitted, "but goat's milk is the only thing that has helped Darcy's nervous stomach."

"I don't see how anyone could keep milk from that foul-smelling animal down," Miss Bell said, her nostrils flaring as Nanny came around the corner of the house. The goat stood with two front feet planted on the porch step and looked curiously at our visitor. Miss Bell set the glass of lemonade on the porch as if she thought it were contaminated. As she started down the steps, she gave Nanny an angry swat with her straw hat. Nanny, who had never been a victim of animal abuse, must have thought that Miss Bell meant to play; Nanny grabbed the hat and took off running.

Darcy caught Nanny on the second high-speed lap around the house, right in front of the furious Miss Bell.

I pulled the hat out of Nanny's mouth. It was a little wet and slightly chewed. Sheepishly I handed it to Miss Bell. With a withering glance she snatched it from me. Holding the hat as if it were covered with ticks and fleas, she marched to her old car. I was just thinking we had probably seen the last of that neighbor for a long time when we heard her shriek of rage. We could see that she was batting at something on the front seat of her car with her hat.

Mother in the lead, we all ran to see what had Miss Bell in such a tizzy. What we saw started Mother shaking with uncontrollable laughter. There, curled up on the car seat and blinking in surprise at all the commotion, was Kid.

"I guess Kid wants to go home with you, Miss Bell," Mother finally stammered between giggles.

"How did Kid ever get the car door open?" I asked.

Miss Bell glowered at me. "I left the door ajar to let some cool air into the car. I see that nothing is safe around this place."

Darcy tugged at Kid, who really was acting as if she wanted to go home with the quarrelsome Miss Bell. No matter how hard Darcy pulled on Kid, she only snuggled closer to the car seat. It was then that Aaron came from the garden with a handful of carrots. Kid, never one to turn down a treat, jumped out of the car and scampered after Aaron.

Miss Bell bounced behind the steering wheel of her car snarling. "You keep those dirty goats away from my place, or you'll be hearing from my lawyer," she warned as she drove away.

Everyone gave a sigh of relief and went inside, talking and giggling over Miss Bell's visit. Only her threat of calling her lawyer sobered me.

"Do you think she will call the law in on us?" I said as we went about our chores.

Mother chuckled. "I doubt if she wants to explain how her belligerent visit to a neighbor turned out so laughably."

One day there was a great clatter on the roof. Mother threw up her hands and ran outside with me close on her heels. What we saw set my stomach churning with fear. There, on the very edge of the roof, was Kid, looking down at us; she had discovered the ladder Aaron had left leaning against the house when he had repaired the screen on the upstairs window the night before.

Mother gets acrophobia two feet off the ground, but in her excitement she did scale enough of the ladder to reach the mischievous goat. Kid, however, didn't want to be reached. With a daring turn she circled the roof again, coming even closer to the edge.

White-faced by now, Mother backed down the ladder.

"Kate, you will have to go up there and get her!"

I had no fear of heights. Going up the ladder was a breeze, and even inching across the roof wasn't too bad, until my baggy jeans got caught on a nail. No matter how much I twisted and turned, the nail held me like a fly in a spider's web.

"Scoot back!" Mother yelled, seeing my sorry plight. "Back up, so the nail can let loose."

I gave a mighty heave backward. The nail held fast, and I let out a yell of pain that sent Kid clattering around the roof again. Mother, sure that I was mortally wounded, forgot her fear of heights and scampered up the ladder like a chipmunk to rescue both her "kids."

Nanny's milk had helped Darcy's nervous stomach, but he was still having his troubles at school. Every week he brought another note from his teacher, informing me of some new episode. Last night it had been about another fight Darcy had been in on the school grounds.

I couldn't understand the teacher's concern. All children had disagreements. Mine had plenty of them at home. I thought of the black eye Darcy had come home with yesterday. My son had evidently gotten the worst of the battle, so why was the teacher sending me a note about the scrap? By rights, it was I who should be angry.

I jerked my one decent sweater over my head and picked up the note. I'd set that teacher straight on a few things today. I didn't have time to write excuses and apologies. I certainly didn't have time to traipse over to the school-house, but that was exactly what I was going to do.

With all the turmoil in my own life, I hadn't taken the time to meet this new teacher Darcy was always praising. In spite of the notes the teacher wrote about Darcy's behavior, Darcy liked him. All I knew about him was that he was a middle-aged widower.

"A shy and lonely man," one neighbor said about him. Not too shy to write notes complaining about his pupils, I thought, reading the note again. "Darcy has been in another scrap; I'd like to talk to you. Could you come to school tomorrow?"

"I'll be there," I thought, "but you are not going to enjoy my visit!"

I was starting to put all men into one category and growing more bitter each day. Not that I didn't have good reasons to mistrust them.

Friends I had known for years started dropping by the farm without their wives with the pretext of offering us help. Men I never dreamed would be unfaithful to their wives asked me out or made indecent suggestions. I was too embarrassed to even discuss it with Mother. She came in from the barn as I was ready to leave for the school-house. She saw the note in my hand and said, "I hope you aren't going to be as rude to Lester Clark as you were to Eric last night. Eric only offered to help," she said evenly. "Maybe you *should* let him talk to Darcy."

"No man is going to bully my son!"

Mother sniffed. "I can't see Eric Johnson bullying anyone."

"Well, I won't be told what to do by any man!"

"I know," Mother giggled. "You probably already have as good a reputation as your children for being quick with a punch."

"I'd like to punch that Lester Clark when I get over to the schoolhouse today; I'll let him know he is paid to teach and not waste his time or mine writing notes."

# Chapter 4

# "Mrs. Scrappy"

It was noon when I reached the schoolhouse. The children were sitting or standing in small groups around the school grounds—some eating their lunch, while others were playing games.

Darcy was standing alone, bouncing a basketball in the dust. He turned scarlet when he saw me and without even a wave of welcome ducked behind a huge maple tree. That really goaded my anger. I flung open the door to the schoolroom and marched straight up to the desk where Lester Clark sat, studying some papers. If he saw me coming, he didn't glance up until I said sharply, "Do you think all I have to do is answer notes or run over to this schoolhouse?"

Clark, an amused smile on his boyish face, slowly pushed back his chair. He was a small man, with a shock of rust-colored hair. When he stood up, his grape-green eyes were on a level with my own. His eyes twinkled like someone had just told him a funny joke.

"Mrs. Gills, I presume. I expected you to be belligerent, but no one mentioned you were beautiful."

For a moment I was flustered. Here was a man who insulted me and gave me a compliment in the same breath.

"Just what is that supposed to mean?" I asked, bristling with suspicion.

"Only that I was warned Darcy's mother was 'Mrs. Scrappy,' " he said, not quite able to hide a grin.

"I don't care what the neighbors say about me, Mr. Clark. I'm here because you seem to think we should discuss my son. Darcy got trounced yesterday; isn't that enough punishment for one sad little boy?"

"I didn't mention punishment, Mrs. Scra—ah—Gills," he stammered. "Did you know Darcy got into that fight because one of the boys called you Mrs. Scrappy?"

"I didn't know what the quarrel was about. I have taught my children to stand up for what they think is right. When they do, I try not to question their judgment. I'm sorry if Darcy felt he had to defend me."

"There are worse faults than having a temper," he said, twirling his desk chair around and practically pushing me into it. He slid onto the corner of his desk, saying, "Darcy is not an aggressive child. In fact, there is a gentle quality about the boy that's a delight to behold. He is filled with compassion for others. The other children tease him. They call him 'Preacher' or 'The Deacon.' "

I had to smile. "Quite a pair," I said, "Mrs. Scrappy and the Parson. Doesn't sound like Darcy acquired any of my personality traits."

Clark looked at me with a frown. "Mrs. Gills, I have come to the conclusion that Darcy is not a belligerent boy; often a child takes his cue from a parent."

I glared at him. "Mr. Clark, if it is *my* character you are trying to improve, you are wasting your time and mine. Now I have work to do." I stood up and threw the note on his desk. "If you write any more of these, deliver them yourself." I slammed the door as I went out, still seeing the amused look on Clark's face.

Darcy was nowhere in sight as I walked back across the schoolyard. I thought of his flush of embarrassment on my arrival. What was wrong with the boy anyway? He must have known I'd come there only to defend him. And last night, when he had brought the note home, he had stood kicking his scuffed boot against the step until I had finished reading it. When I looked up, frowning with irritation, he had said hesitantly, "Mom, do you know that some kids get a licking at home every time they get into a fight at school?"

Had Darcy been trying to tell me something? Was his teacher right when he implied that Darcy was hostile because of me? Anger quickened my step, but when I reached the log over the creek, I sat down and let the tears that were blinding me fall into my hands. The teacher, and, yes, even Eric, thought that I was a tyrant. My son was forced into battles for which he had no heart.

Behind my back the neighbors were calling me Mrs. Scrappy. I had seen my son cringe in embarrassment. Last night he had looked to me for some kind of discipline for acting like a bully, into which I was trying to turn him. I heard again, "Mom, do you know that some kids get a licking at home every time they get into a fight at school?"

Tom's dream had been for less violence in the world, and I had spent all these months since his death fighting with everybody. I wiped my eyes with the back of my hand. My thoughts turned to Eric. I recalled the hurt in his eyes when I had lashed out at him because he had offered to have a talk with Darcy. I felt so guilty. "Dear Lord," I whispered, "I know there will always be problems to overcome and battles to win. I'm afraid my biggest problem is with my ornery self. Please help me win this battle going on within me."

I rose and started again on my trek toward home. Suddenly, I was giggling. No one could handle a fight better than Mrs. Scrappy.

Mother was waiting for me with a twinkle in her eyes when I reached the house. "Here is a critter as feisty as you are," she said, handing me a small wooden crate. I peeked between the slats of the crate at the shiny red-and-black plumage and met the stare of the small bantam rooster.

"He looks like the real angry American!" I gibed.

"Mean is a better word for that one," Mother declared, holding up a bloody finger. "Pecked me good when I got my finger between the slats unloading the crate."

With the warning of, "Watch out for that fierce bundle of pillow stuffing," Mother went inside to doctor her finger.

Hammer in hand, I carried the bantam to the chicken house. The little rooster came out of his prison like an angry bee. With savage strength and squawks of rage, he flew at walls and windows. I held the hammer weapon-style, sure that life and limb were in danger. He ignored me completely until I started out the door. Then, like a flash, he struck the back of my legs, tearing my stockings and drawing blood.

I gave him a kick that set him back on his tail feathers and ran out the door. The first round of our feud had ended in a draw.

At five o'clock the next morning I was jerked off my pillow by the loud flapping of wings and the lusty cry of "Cock-a-doodle-dooo." I ran to the window and looked out.

On the fence below sat the bantam rooster. Somehow he had managed to break out of the chicken house.

As soon as I was dressed, I went outside, hoping to coax the pesky fowl back to the barnyard. He saw me coming and charged as I stepped off the porch. I grabbed up an old broom and lifted him high in the air. He landed on his feet, squawking with anger.

For days I never ventured off the porch without the broom when I saw the little rooster. This seemed to confuse the banty a little, but he only reversed his tactics. Now, instead of meeting me head on, he came sneaking up from the rear.

One morning, after making sure that he was nowhere in sight, I set out, pail of water in one hand and a pan of grain in the other. Suddenly, without warning, the aggressive banty struck me just behind the knees. Water and grain went flying, and I tripped and sprawled in the dust. The banty eyed me warily while pecking at the grain. When

I got to my feet, he backed off a few paces, waxing hostility. I had to laugh.

"You are a real warrior," I said, picking up the empty water pail to swing at him warningly. "I guess I will call you 'Soldat,' my little soldier of fortune."

He cocked his head as if listening. As I walked to the house, he strutted pompously just one step ahead of me.

Soldat was the barnyard Houdini. It was impossible to keep him penned. He called me out of bed at daybreak every morning from his perch on the fence. When I heard the first boisterous crow, I knew I might just as well get up. He never stopped shouting until he heard the slam of the backdoor.

One morning, when I returned home laden with bundles after a two-day business trip in town, I saw Soldat coming to meet me. Oh, dear, I thought, here goes another pair of nylons.

Straight down the path marched Soldat. I flexed my leg muscles in anticipation. Soldat was picking up speed. He sped down the path like an arrow sure of the target. I pulled back my foot ready for a kick at him, but just before he came within range, he stopped. Slowly he danced around muttering happy little sounds of chicken talk.

"You must have really missed me," I said, hoping he had decided on a truce. He stood still, cocking his head. Gingerly, I took a step forward. Soldat turned his back and marched ahead of me to the door. I never had to carry a weapon again. From that day on we were friends.

Soldat still had his enemies. His favorite was Joe Taylor, who liked to stop and talk to Mother.

Joe was a small man with a watermelon stomach and a flat posterior that allowed his pants to droop dangerously low in the seat. One morning he stopped to pick up the six dozen cookies Mother had baked for the church bazaar. As he stepped off the porch with the cookies, Soldat made one of his sneak attacks. His spur got caught in the seat of Joe's sagging trousers.

The cookie-laden Joe screamed like a banshee. He

jumped high in the air, flailing his legs backward. Hanging head down, Soldat squawked in rage. In spite of high jumps, kicks, yells, and loud, angry squawks, Joe and Soldat stuck together until I rescued them.

At the sale, Mother found what we thought would be the perfect wife for Soldat. She was tiny, buff colored, and as dainty as a ballerina. I'm sure Soldat fell in love with her at first sight.

In due time Mrs. Soldat decided to raise a family. When I was sure she was ready to stay on her nest, I slipped six large hen eggs under her.

When the chicks arrived, Soldat acted like any proud father. He would follow them around as his mate led them through the barnyard, strutting a few yards behind. Sometimes, he would call them back to share a bug or worm.

When the chicks were about a month old, Soldat had a change of heart. He turned into a real crank with the little ones and became so greedy that I had to shut the mother and her brood up to feed them.

One night when I was ready to close the door on them, I heard a commotion behind me. There was Soldat, running down the path driving a stray I hadn't even missed. As the lost chick joined the others, Soldat gave me a look that said, "I may be chicken, but I'm not dumb!"

Soldat died as violently as he had lived. One morning, a terrible racket brought me running to the kitchen window.

A large truck was parked at the edge of the road. The driver was coming up the walk carrying a small, bedraggled bantam rooster.

"Sorry," the man said, a perplexed look on his tanned young face. "I blew the air horn and slowed down to a crawl, giving him plenty of time to get out of the way. But this crazy rooster charged right at me. I believe he was trying to attack the truck."

"He probably was," I said with a catch in my voice, as I took the lifeless form of the spunky bantam in my arms. Our brave little warrior had finally tangled with something he couldn't intimidate or whip.

# Chapter 5

# An Unsavory Suitor

One morning, Mother and I were dressing chickens for sale. The children had left for school, and the house was quiet and cozy. A steady drizzle of rain reminded me I was going to get wet when I went to look for the horses. They were missing earlier that morning.

"Why don't you sell those pesky horses?" Mother asked as I pulled on my boots to leave.

"Who would buy those two old plugs except a pet food company? I can't let them end up there."

Like an answer to my question, Mike Marshal drove into our driveway. Mike had never been one of my favorite people. He had a sour disposition and a reputation for liquor and women. I had always felt sorry for his little over-worked wife. When I opened the door, I could tell, early as it was, he had already been tipping the bottle.

"Your horses are tracking up my wheat field," he said belligerently.

"I'm sorry," I apologized. "I'll go and get them at once. Of course I'll pay for any damages," I added.

Marshal's bloodshot eyes squinted at me shrewdly.

"I think I know a fellow who might buy them," he said.

I thought of all the ways we could use the money and of

the damage to his field that I was going to have to pay.

"I would like to sell them," I said.

Marshal stepped off the porch and spit a wad of chewing tobacco into the rose bed. "Well, come on and I'll take you to see the guy and help you get the horses out of my field."

I looked helplessly at Mother, but if I had expected help from her, I saw at once that I could just as well forget it. She gave me that "You're a big girl now" look and went right on picking the chicken.

My mistrust of Marshal was well-founded. An hour later, I stormed back into the kitchen, wet and angry. Mother called to me with a giggle in her voice, "Did you have to walk home?"

"Yes, I did!" I snapped. "That old philanderer had no intention of taking me to see any man interested in the horses."

Mother came into the kitchen. "Honey, I wasn't trying to be funny. I had no idea that Marshal didn't bring you home when I said that."

"Well, he didn't bring me home; the old coot parked up at his wheat field where the horses were and, well—"

I felt my face burn with shame, remembering the encounter with Marshal. "I told him where he could go," I snapped. "Then I brought the horses home."

"Did the horses cause a lot of damage to his field? How much is it going to cost you?" Mother asked, a worried frown between her gray eyes.

"Damage!" I hissed. "Just let that copperhead try and collect for any damage! How about my injured pride? He should pay for that!" I stormed.

Mother put her arm around my shoulders, "Honey, calm down. These things are bound to happen to a woman when her husband is gone. I had hoped it wouldn't start so soon, but a pretty woman brings out the beast in some men. They think you can't get along without a man."

"I'd rather live with a rattlesnake than with a man like Marshal," I said, slamming my fist on the table.

"Be about as safe," Mother sniffed. "Honey, don't let that kind of man turn you into a recluse. A lot of nice, honorable men are left in the world."

I was sure she was thinking about Eric Johnson. I knew she secretly hoped that some day I would see Eric as more than a friend of the family. This was one wish I felt Mother was never going to see come true. Eric was like one of my brothers. Besides, I had no intention of marrying again. The children were my whole life now. Besides, I couldn't see Eric as ever being more than my very best friend. I was sure he felt the same way about me.

That evening, when the children had come home from school, Mother said to Aaron, "We have to watch this mother of yours; she had a date with a horse-trader today and had to walk home."

I knew Mother had thought Aaron would regard this as a big joke, something to tease me about, but the look on Aaron's face at that moment was no joking matter.

Mother realized her mistake. "It wasn't that kind of date, really," she said, hurrying to tell the story. Aaron sat ashen-faced while Mother explained what had happened. When she finished he jumped up from the table.

"I'll beat that Marshal to a pulp!" he said, starting for the door.

I grabbed his arm. "Son, you can't go around beating up every man that tries to get fresh with your mother." I gave him a playful punch on the arm I held. "I think I can take care of myself."

Later I remarked to Mother, "I don't think we better tell Aaron about any of my future encounters with trouble-some men."

"I guess you are right," she said, as we watched him scuff angrily toward the barn with the milk pail.

Mother shook her head. "I really thought he would think it funny. I still see him as a little boy instead of a young man."

My growing resentment toward men was making me overly protective of Wanda. I pondered this the day I glanced out the window just in time to see her land a sharp uppercut on the chin of one of her admirers. The boy spun off the porch with a silly look of surprise on his face. Wanda gave him one last contemptuous look and breezed into the house.

"So, you saw what happened," she said defiantly, seeing me standing at the window.

"Why did you hit him?" I asked, thinking I had better be more careful of what I said about men in the future. I didn't want my daughter to turn into a person who would be unable to accept the sincere love of a future husband.

Wanda tossed her auburn hair away from her pretty face.

"He tried to get clutchy," she said peevishly. "Boys!" she sniffed. "I'd rather kiss my horse than any of them."

"But aren't you afraid of running out of admirers if you keep acting like a boxer?" I teased.

"Who needs them?" she said, slamming out of the room.

"Whatever got into her?" Mother asked, coming through the door as Wanda swept out.

"I'm afraid I have warned her too may times about all the pitfalls in dating without getting across the message that real love can be beautiful," I said wearily.

Mother smiled. "Don't worry. When the right man comes along, our little spitfire will fall in love."

"Didn't you see her clobber her latest boyfriend?" I asked, thinking of the silly look of surprise on the boy's face as he backed off the porch.

"No, but the other day I overheard one of Aaron's friends saying that Wanda has a left hook as good as her brother. Really, Honey, it's not the children's character traits I'm worried about."

Her words took me by surprise. "You don't mean me," I hedged, knowing very well that she did.

"Yes, I mean you. Lately, every time you see a man coming your eyes grow flinty, and your chin juts out stubbornly. I'm glad you don't look as ornery as you act."

"And just what is that supposed to mean?" I asked sullenly.

Mother grinned. "If you looked like you act, you couldn't get away with it."

I felt the sting of tears and swiped at them with the back of my hand. "Don't I have plenty of reason to be on the defensive? My ordeal with Marshal is an example of why I feel under attack and always ready to defend myself."

Mother hugged me around the neck. "I'm sorry, Honey. I wasn't scolding. I just don't like to see my little girl so bitter and disillusioned."

I returned her hug. "Don't worry about me, Mom. I'll survive."

She flashed me her funny little smile, her lower lip stuck out to look stubborn. "Of course you will; you are plowing a straight furrow."

I grinned at her. "Talking about plowing, your fair-haired boy is going to start on ours tomorrow. I saw him when I brought the horses across the field."

Mother looked surprised. "Did you tell him about your fight with Marshal?"

"Of course not," I grunted, and felt the blood rushing up my neck and cheeks. "Don't you dare tell him either."

"Now, now, don't get yourself all upset again; I'm not going to tell him. The man has a wife to be pitied. Sorry I mentioned it in front of the children."

I shrugged. "Don't worry about it. I'm sure they aren't going to tell anyone. They are as embarrassed about it as I am."

"No reason for you to be ashamed, Honey. You didn't do anything wrong."

"Guess you are right," I replied. "I only set out to sell a couple of old horses who seem to think the grass is greener on the other side of the fence."

"I suppose that means we'll have some fence building to do tomorrow," Mother replied.

"Afraid so," I said. "Now we had better get the kids started on the rest of the chores. I'll go up and make my peace with Wanda."

"Peacemaker or slave driver?" Mother teased, pulling on

her old chore coat, a slight smile curving the corners of her mouth.

I knew she was trying to dispel the turbulence within me.

"A little of each," I sighed. "I'm so physically and emotionally drained from all these decisions I have to make each day. I need Tom to lean on and to help me. He always had such a close relationship with the children."

"It couldn't have been any closer than the tie you have with them," Mother replied. "Just remember, Honey, that children can't profit by our mistakes. They mature while making and correcting their own."

I shrugged. "This child of yours is beginning to feel very old from making and trying to correct hers."

Mother's eyes twinkled. "How old do you think I feel? I'm twenty years your senior, and I'm still maturing."

Wanda was lying on her bed, staring at the ceiling. She turned her back to me when I came into the room. I sat down on the bed and put my arm around her.

"Don't shut me out, Honey," I said softly. "We need to talk."

She flopped over on her back and looked at me, her eyes expressing defiance. "Mother, I don't know what I am! I'm not a kid anymore, and I'm not yet ready to be treated as a woman."

"I understand, Dear. I sometimes feel as vulnerable now as I did at your age."

She looked at me closely. "You mean because of what happened when you went to sell the horses?"

"I guess that is one reason, and I find my tongue is foolhardy too. I'm a victim of anxiety, and I try to camouflage my feelings with anger. I'm not a good example for you children to model after."

Wanda slipped her hand into mine. "You are the best mother in the whole world. I want to grow up to be just like you."

"Thanks, Honey," I said past the lump in my throat. "I'm sure things will improve. Remember, the Bible says, 'it came to pass,' not, 'it came to stay'."

## Chapter 6

# Making Ends Meet

When winter came, it was one of the coldest I could remember since living on the farm. Day after day it snowed without stopping. The howling wind piled the snow into six-foot drifts against the house and barn.

During the night the water froze in the bucket in the kitchen. Bedroom floors were like stepping on an ice rink when we got out of bed in the mornings. Outside, our steaming breath froze in our nostrils as we rushed about doing the chores.

Mother added a lot of stars on the old blackboard that winter. I am sure that without her help and encouragement all of us would have been willing to call it quits. When I saw how hard Mother was working to keep us on our slim budget it brought back all the old memories of growing up during the Depression years. At that time, no matter how many things we had to do without, Mother would never admit to being in the poor class.

In those days there were four of us children, and my widowed mother had to raise us with very little money. No matter how small the amount, Mother stretched it to keep us fed and clothed.

Sometimes our payments would be a little late, but our

bills were always paid. Food was plain and clothing scanty, but Mother wouldn't admit that we were poor.

I remember one year just before Christmas, when someone had a big box of things delivered to our house. Mother was at the corner grocery store at the time the large box arrived.

"We don't dare look inside until Mother gets home!" my sister Olive warned, but I was already lifting the rag doll with red yarn hair off a hundred pound sack of flour. There were many cans of food and many layers of clothing; soft sweaters and wool plaid skirts. Knit caps and gloves and black ribbed stockings. I had never seen so many pretty things in one pile before. I had the doll clutched to my bony chest and was wearing one of the plaid skirts when Mother opened the door. She took one look at the huge box sitting in the middle of the room and turned pink with humiliation.

"Who dared to leave that box for the poor at our house?" she demanded.

"We don't know," Olive said quickly. Olive never wanted to get in trouble with Mother. "Two men came, and when I opened the door, they just set the box right there. I didn't get into it, Mother," she said, looking at me spitefully.

"Those men can come and take it straight back," Mother said angrily. "We don't need charity!'

"But, Mother!" I wailed. "Can't we just keep some of it? I love this doll, and see how this skirt twirls out."

I whirled around to make the skirt swing wide.

"Put everything back in that box!" Mother said sternly, jerking the skirt roughly over my ears. "I know that nosey Doctor Harrison is to blame for this," she fumed.

Mother pulled on her old faded green coat as if she were donning armor. As I watched her march off up the street, her back stiff as a poker, I felt rather sorry for our old family doctor. I never knew for sure what Mother said to him. No doubt she convinced him that we were "middle class," because soon the same two men came and took the box away again.

I was the oldest in the family, and although I was sure that we were poor, Mother never once agreed with me. With a toss of her heavy brown hair, she would look me in the eye, saying, "Only those who would rather take a handout than work are in the poor class. We work for what we get."

If work was a reward, Mother was truly blessed. I can't remember ever seeing her idle. Late in the evening when she at last put away her washboard, cooking pots, and broom, she would sink wearily into her old wooden rocker. Her hands would automatically reach for the mending basket. When we grumbled because money was nonexistent and our clothes were faded and patched, Mother reminded us that "patches are honorable, and whatever we need, the Lord will provide."

One day at school, some of the girls made snide remarks about my coat. Grandmother had made that coat for me out of her old one. I thought it was beautiful until the girls made fun of it. That evening I slunk home, head hanging and face tear streaked. Mother saw me coming and met me at the door.

"Whatever is wrong, Darling?" she cooed, pulling me inside.

I pulled away and jerked off the detestable coat. Throwing it on a chair, I stamped my foot. "I hate it! I hate it!" I shouted. "I will never wear it again. Never, never, never!"

Mother's gentle concern vanished. "Of course you will wear the coat again," she said firmly. "It was fashioned lovingly just for you, and you will wear it with pride. And you hold your head up proudly, too, Young Lady," she warned. "The only time this family walks humbly is with the Lord."

"I hate being in the poor class," I sobbed.

"You are in the middle class," Mother said, picking up the coat. "If you were in the poor class you would be wearing some stranger's coat given to you." She brushed her hand across the coat sleeve tenderly. "This coat is all family. It is strictly middle class," she said, handing me the coat.

One summer, Mother helped a farmer's wife during harvest in exchange for the knots and limbs of trees that were going to waste on their farm. Early each morning we would take gunnysacks and go gather fuel. One day when the five of us were returning tired and dusty with our bulging sacks, we came face to face with Mrs. Grahm, the banker's wife, and her son, David.

I had had a secret crush on David for a long time. Now, I wished the ground would open up and swallow me and that awful sack of sticks. Mrs. Grahm stopped to chat with Mother. I stood there twisting the ear of my sack, trying to look any place except at David Grahm.

"Where did you ever find those nice pitch fagots?" Mrs. Grahm gushed.

Very much at ease, Mother explained about the work she had supplied for the right to gather the wood.

"I just know you don't have any trouble getting a fire to burn with that kind of wood," Mrs. Grahm said. "The last wood my husband bought is so green that I have a terrible time getting a fire to burn."

"Take these," Mother said, tugging the sack out of my clenched hand and handing it over to Mrs. Grahm.

Mrs. Grahm accepted the sack like it held gold nuggets. "This is really nice of you, Mrs. Lewis," she said, pushing the sack over to her son to carry. "Tomorrow, David can go along and fill another sack for you."

David hoisted the sack to his shoulders, pretending to stagger under the weight. Then he winked at me. "Guess we have a date to go fagot hunting tomorrow."

"Guess so," I gulped, knowing just how Cinderella must have felt when the prince slipped the glass slipper on her foot.

The next time I muttered something about being in the poor class, Mother scoffed, "What do you mean, poor class? Would the banker's son gather fagots with a pauper's daughter? Of course not," she declared, answering her own question. "Bankers are strictly middle class."

"Oh, Mother, you know the Grahms are rich and upper class."

"Phooey," Mother sniffed. "Have they got a million dollars? Are they as rich as Rockefeller or Ford?"

"Well, no," I had to admit.

"You see," Mother said smugly, "same as us—middle class."

Now my Mother was working just as hard to help me keep another generation "middle class."

One day, not long before Christmas, Mother read somewhere that a burro ate much less than a horse. At once she decided a burro was the perfect gift for Darcy.

Coming home from the next barn sale, Mother was followed by John Martin and his truck, delivering the burro for her. Because our lane was soggy and wouldn't accommodate the heavy truck, John and the burro arrived on foot.

"Did you buy this long-eared creature for a plow?" John asked me, tugging on the rope around the burro's neck. The burro inched forward on stubbornly braced feet, pushing a layer of mud before it.

"Mother bought the burro to give to Darcy for Christmas," I explained.

John handed me the rope and left, shaking his head. The burro, as if in agreement with him for the first time, also shook its head and began such irritating braying that I nearly fell off the porch. The noise brought Darcy running out of the house. Darcy started at once to beg for a ride. Grandma took the problem right in hand.

"The burro is your Christmas gift, Darcy, but you can't ride it until your mother has ridden him around first to make sure it's safe for you," she said firmly.

"You don't mean me!" I said disbelievingly, knowing fullwell that she did, and thinking how stupid I was going to look up on the back of an animal that resembled an old fur coat from some mission barrel. "We will wait until Aaron gets home. I can't ride that—that ignoble beast."

Mother avoided looking at me. Her gaze rested reverently on the Christmas scene she and Darcy had painted across the front window of our house. In this painting a very famous person was riding a mount closely resembling our new burro.

"Some very important people have been known to ride upon what you choose to call an ignoble beast," she said sarcastically.

I felt my face burn. "Oh, for Pete's sake," I mumbled. "Wait until I get into some jeans, and I'll ride that soulful-eyed beast."

Mother and Darcy huddled on the back porch, trying to stay out of the wind, while I spent the next five minutes shouting, "Get up! Get up!" My mount only hunched up and leaned forward with his feet braced. After a few minutes of the burro's moving only in his hide. I was almost on his long ears.

I was slowly moving back to the burro's middle, determined that when I got back there, I would do more than shout, when Darcy slapped a paper sack he had been blowing into. The sack burst with a bang any gun would have been proud of. It was then that the burro and I violently parted company. Upon hearing the sack explode, the burro gave one unexpected leap that carried us under the clothesline. As I was floating back to earth, the clothesline caught me just under the arms and for one awful moment, I hung there like a piece of laundry. Suddenly, the clothesline, the line post, and I, landed all wrapped up together in one unsightly heap.

Mother rushed from the porch. "Are you hurt?" she asked, helping me to my feet. Not being able to find a single scratch didn't help my bad temper. "It's no thanks to you and your blasted burro that I'm not dead," I stormed.

Mother looked at me helplessly. "I guess I made a bad buy," she said sadly. "I'll list the burro for sale in the paper tomorrow."

This brought a wail of disappointment from Darcy, but the ad came out in the next paper just the same.

Two days later a man came to see if we still had the burro for sale. I assured him that we did and led the way to the barn. Triumphantly, I flung open the barn door. There, to my dismay, standing as docile as a lamb, was the burro with Darcy on his back.

"This man has come to buy the burro," I said, and more bedlam couldn't have broken loose if I'd said the world was coming to an end in five minutes.

The cries and wails brought Mother hurrying from the house. She took one look at the tear-streaked Darcy still astride the sad-eyed burro and cooed, "Isn't that sweet, Kate? You can't still want to sell the burro."

I looked at the prospective buyer. The man shrugged his shoulders, and said with resignation, "I guess you no longer have a burro for sale. Seeing that little boy on it, I don't think I'd have bought it anyway."

So, in spite of the mangy beast that always looked like he would like to hang me on a clothesline again, Darcy got a burro for Christmas.

## Chapter 7

# Christmas

Two days before Christmas, Darcy and his beloved "Gram" started off to town for the final shopping. There would be no money for fancy gifts this year, but Gram had busied herself for weeks making something for everyone. Now, she would buy the few things that we couldn't grow to make her planned feast a success. I was thankful my sister Olive and her husband Edward would be coming for Christmas. I knew that Mother missed her other daughter, and no one could be unhappy very long with my bubbly sister around.

It was almost dark when Mother and Darcy returned home. A blast of cold winter wind came in with them each time they returned with another load of goodies from the pickup.

"I hope this weather doesn't get so bad that Edward and Olive won't be able to get out here," I said, as Mother set a bag of oranges on the kitchen table. Darcy was racing off for another load from the pickup.

"Oh, they'll be here. Olive is like Santa Claus—she will come if she has to get a red-nosed reindeer. Speaking of Santa Claus, I think it's time you told Darcy there really isn't one."

I frowned. "Mother, you know I've always told the children there is no real Santa Claus. Didn't Darcy behave today?" I asked, thinking what I would do to the young man if he had caused his grandmother any trouble.

"Oh, he wasn't misbehaving," Mother said with a chuckle. "In fact, he had my best interest in mind when he sidled up to a Santa Claus in the crowded department store and said loud and clear, 'Santa, for Christmas please bring Grandma a manure spreader!' "

"He didn't!" I exclaimed, sure she was making a joke. She grinned. "He did, and later when I asked him why, he said that Eric had a manure spreader, and it sure looked a lot easier when he fertilized his field than the way we had to do ours."

"I believe our little Darcy has a small lazy streak," I replied. "He is always trying to figure out an easier way to do a chore, or he gets his nose in a book and forgets the job completely."

Mother looked thoughtful. "I've been meaning to talk to you about Darcy and his books. Have you noticed the books he reads? They are all religious. That first book of Bible stories I gave him when he was five is so worn it looks more like a rag than a book. When he isn't reading it, he just carries it around the way you carried that old pink teddy bear around for your security blanket when you were small."

I grinned, thinking about my old teddy bear. Mother never could believe I really remembered her making booties for Olive out of it when I was three years old. The bear had already lost its head and one leg before it disappeared. But when I first saw the little pink booties on my sister's feet, I knew they were my beloved bear.

Mother was still looking thoughtful. "I bought Darcy a new book of Bible stories today."

"I thought we agreed not to buy gifts this year," I said.

"I know," Mother replied, not meeting my indignant stare.

"I didn't buy anything for the other children."

"Mother, you spoil Darcy. He would be just as happy with gloves and a cap like you made for Aaron and Wanda."

"Aaron and Wanda are different," Mother replied. "Maybe because they are closer in age and have each other to share things with. Darcy is a loner. I admit it's often his preference, and it may not be a wrong choice."

"Mother, are you trying to tell me something?"

Mother looked at the oranges she was arranging in a bowl. "I think we should start saving a little each month toward an educational fund for Darcy. I'd like to see him go to the academy when he is ready."

"Mother, we can't afford to send Darcy to a private school. We can hardly keep the children clothed and in public school."

"The Lord will provide," Mother said, setting the bowl on the table with a flourish. "Did you see Eric today?" she asked, changing the subject.

"For a minute," I replied. "He brought some packages and put them under the Christmas tree."

"Did you invite him for Christmas dinner?"

"Oh, you won't believe this," I said, remembering the bit of news I had been so anxious to impart before she returned from town. "Eric is having Christmas dinner at Miss Bell's house."

Mother smiled. "I'm not really surprised."

"What do you mean, you are not surprised? Can you imagine having dinner with Miss Bell when you could have spent the day with a houseful of friends?"

"Did Eric tell you why he is having dinner with Miss Bell?"

"He said she had invited him, and he knows she gets lonely."

"Well, there is your answer. You see, Eric has more compassion than we have. We should have invited Miss Bell to our house for Christmas dinner."

"Oh, Mother, perish the thought; besides, Miss Bell thinks we are all contaminated around here. Remember her last visit?"

Mother grinned. "How can I forget? I thought she was going to beat poor Kid to death with her hat before we could get the goat out of her car."

"I am glad Kid survived," I said. "She is going to be a mother."

"Oh, dear, another Kid for the roof," Mother said and grinned. Then she added, "I do wish I had invited Eric before Miss Bell gave him that invitation though."

"I'm surprised you didn't," I said.

Mother looked at me intently. "Honey, I wasn't sure you would approve, since you didn't even want to celebrate the holidays at all this year."

"I don't know that Eric being here for dinner would make the day special; he eats half his meals here anyway. You spoil him as much as you do Darcy."

Mother looked serious. "Kate, think of all Eric does to help us. How can you be so malicious?"

"Oh, all right, I'm sorry. I know Eric is a good person. When he finds out Darcy thinks you should have a manure spreader, he will probably give you his for Christmas."

Mother chuckled and tossed a piece of hard candy into my lap. "Sweeten up your disposition, Honey," she said, pouring the rest of the candy into a dish.

Darcy was astride his burro when Edward and Olive arrived on Christmas morning. "Auntie, I got a Christmas burro," he shouted as Olive stepped out of the car. "It only bucks when Mom rides it," he said with a wide grin. "You can ride it right now," he said, slipping off the shaggy back of the little beast.

We all laughed as Olive, who has legs a lot longer than mine, eyed the burro. Finally, she gave Darcy a hug, saying, "Honey, if I ride today, I'll get snow on my boots. I think I'll wait until next Christmas. Maybe your burro will grow a little taller by then."

Darcy was right about the burro bucking only when I rode it. All three of the children had been on it since then, and not once had the burro been anything but nice and docile. Of course, no one had popped a paper bag when the others were riding it.

The aroma of turkey and pumpkin pie greeted us as we entered the kitchen. Mother had the table set, and soon we were gathered around it. As the happy sounds of eager voices rose and fell around me, my thoughts wandered back to Tom and all the holidays we had spent around this old oak table. Christmas had always been a close family time. "We are still a family," I told myself sternly and tuned back into the conversation in time to hear Olive ask Wanda about her plans for the future.

"Wanda, have you thought of what you will do after you graduate from high school this spring?"

"No," Wanda replied. "Not really. I'll get a job, of course."

"How would you like to go to beauty school?" Olive inquired.

Wanda's eyes lighted up. "I'd love to be a beautician just like you, Auntie." Then she shrugged. "I don't have money to go to beauty school," she said resignedly.

"I'll take care of that part," Olive said. "It will be your graduation gift from me."

"I can't let you do that, Olive," I said. "Maybe by spring our finances will improve."

Olive grinned at me. "Kate, just how are you going to stop me from giving my only niece a graduation gift of my choice?" she demanded with all the old fire I remembered when we were quarreling children.

"You haven't changed a bit, Little Sister," I chided her. "You never did let me win an argument."

"I'm not going to start now," Olive said with a grin and gave me a playful kick under the table. "I'm not getting any younger," she said. "I'll be wanting to cut back my workload before long. It will be nice to have someone I can trust and depend on in my shop."

I looked into my daughter's shining eyes and knew I was once again a witness to another of God's plans for my little family.

# Chapter 8

# The Doctor's Proposal

One evening I received a phone call from Dave Garon. I hadn't heard from Dave since Tom's funeral. Now he was asking me to go with him to a dinner honoring the ones who would soon be full-fledged chiropractors. I thought of how Tom had always teased Dave. "Old Garon has too much smart to hang around us country bumpkins," he would say every time Dave came to visit.

Now Dave was saying, "Kate, I want to take someone special to this dinner. Don't disappoint me. Just say you will go with me."

"I'm not sure. I haven't been going out since Tom's death except with the children."

"We have been friends for a long time," Dave said. Still I hesitated. I thought of some of Tom's other friends and remembered all my grievances.

"Kate, are you still there?"

"Yes," I replied. "Just give me some time to think about this."

"Only until tomorrow," Dave replied. "I will call you then."

I was still sitting by the phone in deep thought when Mother came into the room.

"Waiting for the phone to ring?" she teased.

"It just rang," I said, feeling a little silly. "I've been invited to a formal dinner."

"A formal dinner," she said, looking prissy. "My, aren't we getting fancy."

I grinned at her. "I'm not being funny; it really is a formal dinner. An old school friend of Tom's, who has been studying to be a doctor, has invited me."

"A doctor," Mother said thoughtfully. "Well, I guess it's a good idea to have a doctor for a friend. You never know when you or some of the family might need one."

I had to laugh. My dear practical Mother—she was priceless. "I haven't said I'm going."

"Of course you are going. It will do you good to go out with your friends. It's the only normal life to live."

"Oh, I'm doing OK without men. Besides, I don't have a dinner dress," I hedged.

"We'll just have to see that you get one!"

"Buy a fancy dress when the kids are wearing patched jeans?"

"Only the fabric, Dear. I'll make the dress."

"Fabric costs money too."

"Don't worry about the money. I still have the cash from the quilt I sold at the sale."

A week later she and the children watched me leave, wearing her lovely creation.

Dave Garon was a small, clean-cut man with a boyish grin and spaniel eyes. I knew that he had married a girl while very young. I had heard Tom say many times, "I don't think poor old Dave will ever get over the hurt of that woman walking out on him."

I had a lovely time at the dinner. Dave was witty and fun to be with. Even the good-night kiss I was dreading never materialized.

Aaron was waiting for me when I came down the stairs the next morning. "Did you and that *quack* have a good time?" he asked sullenly.

Ordinarily I would have reprimanded him for his behavior, but seeing the bewildered little boy behind his struggle for composure, I only frowned at him. "Why do you think Dave won't be a good doctor?"

He looked at me with a glum expression. "Eric said that most chiropractors are quacks."

"Eric should watch his mouth," I said sharply. "I'm sure Dave will be a conscientious doctor." I knew that Eric had lost faith in the medical profession, after watching his mother's suffering all those years, but he had no right to belittle my friends. I sat down at the kitchen table.

"Aaron, I know you think I'm being disloyal to your father."

Aaron's lips trembled. He sat down and covered his face with his hands.

"Darling," I said softly, "I can't keep living in the past. You know I loved your father. There will never be anyone that can take his place in my heart." For a time there was only the sound of the kettle boiling on the back of the stove. Then Aaron lifted his tear-streaked face.

"Well," he said defiantly, "that Dave is smaller than I am. If you marry him, I'll just tell *him* to get wood for the stove and milk the cows!"

I had to laugh. I got up and put my arm around his shoulders. "You don't have to worry about my getting married, Honey. I've got children to raise." I could feel the tension leave his body. For a second he sagged against me with relief, then he jumped up and grabbed the milk pails and slammed out the door. His tuneless whistle drifted back to me as I watched him lope down the path to the barn.

Aaron need not have worried about Dave's becoming his stepfather. The next day I received a letter that made me decide not to go out with him again. Mother was watching me when I looked up after reading it.

"From the look on your face, that must be quite a letter."

I grinned at her. "I've been given an alternative. Little Dave would like to have me for his steady girl, but if I'm not interested, he doesn't want me to trifle with his affections."

Mother sniffed. "Are those doctor's orders?"

I opened the folded sheet of paper and read it to her:

Dear Kate:

These few words are not to place you under any obligation, but I had such a good time last night. Thanks for accepting my invitation. You did me proud, Kate, and even though I may never have the opportunity of another dinner with you, I shall remain forever grateful.

There has been so little time for pleasure since I started my studies. I am thankful for the fact that patience has been perhaps my greatest virtue—it has served me well. This virtue is nourished by the hope that I may soon gain a secure future by sacrificing now. More to the truth—I have been hiding from the part of life so many of us are forever searching for. Hiding from love. Not from desire, but willingly avoiding being exposed. Then comes a distinctive event, and I feel I want a special guest. So, I reach for the telephone and call you. Do I get exposed? What are the symptoms? Sure, Doc knows about them, only he would like to have the diagnosis a little plainer. This is one time he might like to be his own patient, but he is afraid. He knows no cure for this has been found, once it gets a hold of you, unless the one you got it from is willing to stick around and help you over the rough spots. Strange, how serious this love germ can be, and so many people get it—BIG, GROWN-UP people!!!

So here is what I would like to do. I would like to walk through all the four seasons with you at my side. Listen to all your dreams and share mine with you. I'd like to know that when my busy day is over, you will be waiting for me. Kate, I'm asking if we could spend the rest of our lives together. I leave it up to you. If you think you are immune to this disease I have been so afraid of, I would rather not be exposed again. I know it can be almost fatal if a person has it alone. So—I leave it up to you. Write when you have made up your mind about this. In the meantime, I'll be content accepting the envious compliments on my lovely date from my friends at school.

Love,
Dave.

Mother let out her breath as if she had been holding it all the time I was reading. "That's quite a letter," she said, looking at me closely. "There is a man who knows what he wants, and I would say he is being very honest with you."

"Yes, and I intend to be just as honest with him. I will tell him thanks, but I am not interested," I replied, putting the letter back in the envelope. I saw a little smile touch the corners of Mother's mouth. I couldn't resist taunting her. "That doesn't mean your fair-haired boy next door has any better chance either. He had better stop talking about my friends in front of the children too. Did you know he told Aaron that Dave would probably be a quack doctor?"

Mother laughed. "I'd say Eric was jealous."

"Oh, Mother, how often do I have to tell you Eric only thinks of me as a friend. He wouldn't be jealous if I went out with a king."

Mother giggled. "Guess we will never know about that, will we? As for Eric, we'll see," she said, as the children entered the room.

"What are we going to see?" Wanda asked, with a lazy yawn.

"How your mother handles her love life," Gram answered.

I saw the anxiety leap into Aaron's eyes for the second time that morning. "Your grandma is daydreaming," I said hurriedly. "I'm doing all right with my life just as it is. I have no desire for or intentions of making any changes."

Mother looked at me over the top of her glasses. "Not even if you find love again?"

Aaron frowned. "Gram, how do you know when you are in love or if you have found the right person?"

Gram sat down in her favorite old rocker and gave Aaron a look of scrutiny that caused him to blush from ear to ear.

"You getting romantic ideas?" she asked.

"Well, n-n-no," Aaron stuttered. "I just wondered how you know when you've found the right girl."

Gram looked very serious. "First, you forget those fairy tales about falling in love at first sight. Those kinds of feelings can change from day to day. When you think you have found the right one, you take plenty of time to pray and let God lead you. It takes three to make a good marriage: you, your chosen one, and God. A marriage can't grow in magnitude without God's blessing."

Wanda looked thoughtful. "Gram, are you saying people have to be of the same faith to have a happy marriage?"

"I'm not saying it's impossible, but it is more than a little difficult when married people look in different directions. If you are strangers in your religious beliefs, you can't plow a straight furrow. One of you will always be looking back, fearful or resentful of the other's salvation."

Aaron chuckled. "Gram, you are always talking about plowing a straight furrow."

Gram smiled and said, "You see, we seldom change. If there are things about a person that bother you, don't expect love to make the problems go away. We all have some faults we keep forever."

Darcy, who had been taking in all the conversation, spoke up. "Gram, how come *you* don't have any faults?"

At that moment I'm sure she didn't. The face she turned to him was angelic. "Bless you, Honey," she said, reaching out to hug him. "Your old gram has her share of faults. You look at me through the eyes of love and don't see them." Then she giggled. "It's kind of like putting blinders on a horse."

Wanda sniffed. "I doubt if I will ever look at a boy through the eyes of love."

Gram grinned at her. "Honey, when you find that special one, you will know how easy it is to see only the good in a person."

# Chapter 9

# Growing Pains

As if to make up for the bitter cold of winter, our first days of spring were as warm as summer. In late May we were enjoying fresh vegetables from our garden. One morning, Mother and I were out on the front porch shelling sweet, tender peas, when we saw Miss Bell's old Ford chugging up the lane.

"Better count the goats," I told Darcy, who was on the step reading from his new book of Bible stories. "I can't think of anything but a wayward goat that would bring Miss Bell calling on us."

Mother set her pan of peas on a stool between our chairs and got up to welcome our visitor. "Nice to see you again, Miss Bell," she said warmly, placing a chair for her on the shady side of the porch. Miss Bell sat down gingerly in the battered lawn chair. "What brings you out this early in the morning?" Mother asked, picking up her pan of unshelled peas.

Miss Bell looked a little sheepish. "It has something to do with your goats again."

I looked sharply at Darcy. "The goats are all here, Mom," he said quickly and went on with his reading.

"Must be some other neighbor's goats this time, since

53

ours are all here," I said.

"I didn't say anything about the goats being rampant," Miss Bell replied, and I thought I saw a grin trying to replace her expression of sternness when she added, "I want to buy one of them."

I almost dropped the pan of peas I'd picked up to take inside. Miss Bell hurried to explain. "Doctor Mason says I have an ulcer. I remembered you said the goat milk cured the boy's bad stomach."

For a moment I saw Mother bristle slightly with indignation. I surmised she was remembering Miss Bell flailing our poor Kid with her hat. But Mother is an old softy who never turns from anyone who has a problem.

"I guess we could let you have Nanny," she said thoughtfully. "I think she is gentle enough for you to manage." Then she grinned. "I think we will always keep Kid for the roof."

Our visitor looked perplexed. "Kid on the roof?"

Mother chuckled. "Goats climb a lot, Miss Bell, but we will let you discover all their charming habits for yourself since you are going to own one."

Miss Bell fastened her penetrating gaze on Darcy.

"What are you reading there, Boy?"

"Bible stories," Darcy replied, his face beaming. "Grandma gave me this book for Christmas." He stood up and handed over his prize for Miss Bell's inspection.

The woman skimmed through the pages, stopping to look closely at the pictures.

"I miss reading the Bible," she said thoughtfully. "My old eyes can't read the fine print for long. I miss reading a lot." She handed the book back to Darcy, looking him over like she had him under a magnifying glass.

"Do you know how to milk a goat?"

"Yes, Ma'am," Darcy answered.

"How would you like the job of milking the one your Grandma is going to sell to me?"

Darcy looked at me for approval. Miss Bell saw my hesitation. "I could pay him enough to make it worth his time," she said quickly.

I shrugged. "I guess it would be all right now that school will soon be out. Darcy isn't much for farm work around here, but maybe he can put his books aside long enough to milk your goat."

Miss Bell glanced at Darcy again. Her face softened as if she were pleased at what she saw. "Maybe you could bring your book when you come to milk; you might even read some of your Bible stories to me. I'd pay you for your time, of course."

Darcy's eyes danced with excitement. "Could I, Mom?" he pleaded.

"Of course you may read for Miss Bell, but I don't want her to pay you for it. God's words are free for everyone to hear."

"I know, Mom. I like to read my stories to anyone who will listen."

"Will miracles never cease?" I said, as Miss Bell drove out of the yard.

"Never," Mother intoned softly.

On the day when we started our first cutting of hay, the sun blazed down on us with a scorching heat that sent small rivers of perspiration cascading off our brows.

I had noticed at breakfast that Aaron had something on his mind. Since he had failed to bring it up, I surmised he wanted to discuss it with me when we were alone. I had learned to read these signs, and this time I was right again. I'd barely got the rake stopped when he said, "Mom, I want to get my driver's permit this summer."

"You are too young to start gallivanting around in a car."

"Gallivanting," he sneered. "That word went out of style in Gram's age."

I snapped one of the red suspenders that kept my jeans from falling down at my feet. "Since when have we gone in for style around here?"

He grinned. "Mom, I only want to get my learner's permit, so I'll be ready to drive when school starts next fall."

"And what is wrong with the school bus?" I asked.

"I thought I'd sign up to play football next fall. I'll need a car to get home after practice."

"Gram or Wanda can pick you up if you insist on playing. I was hoping you wouldn't. It's a rough game. Your father lived with a bad knee from an old football injury."

"Oh, Mom, I could fall out of the haymow and hurt my knee."

"You don't have much choice with the hayloft since we are farmers, but you don't need to play ball."

Aaron kicked at a clod of dirt. "Mom, you'll never see me old enough to do anything but follow your orders."

I handed him the reins and pushed the damp hair off his forehead. "I order you to unhitch this team and head to the house for lunch," I said in a gruff voice, trying to tease him into a better mood.

Grinning, he started to unhitch the horses, but I knew that the subject was not closed. I was beginning to feel like a villain in the children's lives. Often I'd heard Aaron warn Wanda or Darcy with, "Better knock it off ! Here comes the colonel!"

Mother had lunch on the table when we came in. She mentioned we should deliver Martha Webber's chickens that afternoon.

"Think I'll let you and Darcy go without me today; I have things I'd rather do."

Mother frowned. "You know Mrs. Webber's mother is fond of you, Kate. I heard her say to Martha when we left the last time we were there, 'That Kate Gills has grit and determination.' "

"She probably meant I am stubborn and belligerent. Remember, the neighbors think of me as Mrs. Scrappy!"

Mother looked at me with a twinkle in her eyes. "Whose fault is that?"

I had to laugh. "Oh, you win, Mother. I'll go. Aaron worked hard this morning. He can use an hour or so off this afternoon."

Mother looked thoughtfully at Aaron. She knew how

much he wanted to start driving. "Maybe it's time you let Aaron start his driving lessons. He could run some of these errands for us."

I saw the look of gratitude Aaron flashed his beloved grandmother.

"I've been telling Mom that some farm kids get special driving permits," Aaron said.

"Fifteen is entirely too young to go ripping around the countryside in an automobile," I said shortly.

Mother grinned roguishly. "I wonder if that was the reason your father made you drive that old plug we used to have when you were Aaron's age? Do you remember the time you borrowed his spirited mare without his knowledge and rode to your friends to show off?"

"I remember," I said. "The mare got scared and dumped me in a mud puddle. I had a mile to walk home. When I saw the horse had arrived at home before I did, I was sure Father was going to skin me alive."

Aaron grinned. "Did Grandpa skin you, Mom?"

"No, he was waiting for me on the step. He just reached out and put his arms around me. Then he laughed. Yes, he laughed until the tears ran down his cheeks." I glanced across the table at Aaron. "I know why my father laughed; it wasn't because I looked like I'd spent the afternoon wallowing with the pigs. My father laughed because he was so thankful I was home safe."

Aaron looked down at his plate. "Mom, I know you worry, but I have to learn sometime."

I sighed. "Well, you had better study the driver's training book while we are gone; I guess it's time." Aaron was beaming, and he waved the driver's manual at us as we drove away with Mrs. Webber's chickens nervously peeping in our ears.

My own little chicks were growing up too fast.

## Chapter 10

# Life's Necessities

I gave the faded jeans another careful inspection. I hadn't missed any rips, but there were some dangerously thin spots. No wonder I'd seen Darcy testing their seat-strength in front of the full-length mirror.

Threadbare clothing wasn't the only reason I felt guilty about not getting a steady job in town. There were so many other things I had to deny the children. Like the new bike Mrs. Larson had bought for her son David. Darcy's eyes had lighted up when he told me about it.

Mrs. Larson was only an acquaintance, but I knew her son like my very own. He spent more time at our house than he did at his. He and Darcy were closer than paste and wallpaper.

The door slammed, announcing Darcy's arrival from school. *Lord, please show me the way to give my children the real necessities of life,* I prayed silently as I went down stairs.

Darcy was helping himself to the chocolate cake I had baked that morning. "How was school today?" I asked, replacing the cake cover.

"All right," he replied, slipping onto the kitchen stool and stuffing his mouth with cake. I was surprised when he suddenly said, "Let's go horseback riding."

"You know I can't ride. Remember what happened when I got onto your burro? Why didn't you bring David to go with you?"

"He's out riding his new bike," Darcy answered as he studied the scuffed toe of his boot.

My heart raced. I had asked God for a sign. Was this shabby, disappointed boy my answer? Well, tomorrow I would start looking for a job in town. We certainly could use a steady income around here. Darcy's coaxing interrupted my thoughts. "Come on, Mom, I'll show you how to ride 'Old Pard.'" He grinned at me. "You won't fall off, because Old Pard won't move that fast."

I groped for an excuse but could find no real reason not to go. Mother was at the sale, and Wanda and Aaron wouldn't be home for a couple of hours. "Well, go bridle the horses," I said reluctantly. "When you get your mind set on something, it's easier to agree with you."

He jumped off the stool and planted one of his rare shy kisses on my cheek. "Mom, you're swell."

I brushed up the cake crumbs, then pulled on one of my husband's old shirts. "The things I do to please your children," I whispered past the lump in my throat. For a second the shirt seemed to hang like a hug around my shoulders. I heard Darcy coming up the lane with the horses. I brushed a sleeve across my tear-filled eyes and went out the door.

Darcy tied his horse to the fence and led Old Pard over to me. "How will I ever get on?" I asked.

"Like this," Darcy said, grabbing a handful of mane and swinging himself up. He slipped off and waited for me to follow his example. With quaking knees and gritted teeth, I took a handful of the horse's coarse mane. I gave what I thought was a terrific leap. My feet came only a few inches off the ground. Out of the corner of my eye I saw Darcy bent over with laughter.

I scowled at him. "What's so funny."

Darcy sobered. "Here, let me boost you up." He grabbed

me around the knees and gave a heave that sent me almost over the horse's back. I hung like a sack of meal—my hands closer to the ground than my feet.

"Sit up!" Darcy yelled.

"I can't," I screamed. "I'm too far over." I felt myself slipping and dug my knees into the horse's side for balance. That was a mistake. Old Pard took it as a signal to get going. I could see the ground coming up to meet me. "Darcy!" I shouted. "I'm falling. Quick, drag me back!"

There was a firm grip on my ankles and a mighty jerk. Darcy and I hit the ground together. "Are you hurt?" I asked when I had enough breath to talk.

"No, we just need a derrick to get you on that horse."

"Well, you can't say I didn't try," I said, getting up and brushing the dust from my jeans.

"I've got it!" Darcy exclaimed, jumping to his feet.

"Climb up on the fence, Mom. Then you can step right over the horse's back."

Gingerly, I climbed up on the fence, and Darcy led Old Pard alongside. Teetering dangerously, I extended one leg. When it was almost over, I discovered it was the wrong leg. By the time I got that one back and the other foot off the fence, Old Pard had moved over. I couldn't even touch him with my foot. I was forced to get both feet back on the fence in a hurry or fall on my face in the dust. Darcy pursed his lips and shook his head.

"I'll stand in front of the horse so he can't move," he said, leading Old Pard back to the fence. "And, Mom, don't take so long to get on this time!"

Old Pard was in position with Darcy's young shoulders planted against him. Shaking like a leaf on a limb, this time I landed on the horse's back with a jarring whack.

Darcy grinned and swung onto his own mount. The horses set off at a brisk trot that kept me bouncing like a rubber ball. In time, Darcy looked back. Seeing my plight, he slowed his mount to a walk. I was happy to see that Old Pard was willing to follow suit.

The new pace was much better, and I was able to relax

a little. The sun was going down. A cool breeze came up and fanned my hot brow. I looked at my son's happy face, and a feeling of peace stole over me.

"Mom," he said, "do you know that we've already ridden a mile?"

I laughed. "Better make mine two. I've gone your mile and another one up and down."

Darcy chuckled. "Mom, you're keen."

I couldn't have been happier if he had said I was a queen. Back at the gate he gave me a hug as I tumbled off into his arms.

"Don't you just love our living out here in the country and having fun together?" he asked.

"You could have a lot more if I went to work. I have decided to try and find a job in town," I said, leaning my cheek against his sun-streaked hair.

"I don't want you to ever do that," he said quickly.

"I could buy you a bike like David's if I had a job," I pointed out.

He flashed me an elfish grin. "Mom, watching you get on a horse is more fun than riding David's bike. Can David go with us next time?"

At the mention of a next time, I groaned but said bravely, "I don't see why not, if he can ride a burro!"

He gave me another hug. "I know one thing for sure," he said.

"What's that?" I asked.

"David would give his new bike any day to have his mom spend more time with him. The reason he got the bike was so he wouldn't bother you."

"Tell David he is no bother," I said firmly. Then, with my legs still contoured after Old Pard's sides, I walked toward the house.

Suddenly, I realized the truth of what the Bible teaches about material things. Nothing is more important than caring and being there for those you love. Without knowing it, I *was* giving my children the real necessities of life. And it was a good life.

## Chapter 11

# Things That Go Bump in the Night

Shortly after Aaron got his driver's permit, a new deputy was hired to work the night shift in our small town. From the neighbors and friends, we were hearing a lot of negative stories about the new officer. Some said he had a real grudge against young people.

One evening after school, Wanda and Aaron came home bristling with anger. Aaron didn't even ask, "What's for dinner?" Instead, he jumped up on the kitchen stool, sputtering, "That stupid new deputy came to school assembly today and told us that anyone caught out after curfew would be taken straight down to juvenile court. He said that included anyone coming home after the ballgames without parents or guardians."

"Mom, you will just have to start going with us again," Wanda said, helping herself to one of the cookies Mother had just taken from the oven.

Mother looked at me. "That's a good idea," she agreed. "It will do your mother good to get out and see people again."

Tom and I had always enjoyed the school sports, but the thought of going without him set my heart to racing with panic.

I looked at Mother. "You drive, and I don't. Looks like

you will have to take the children."

"Wanda has her license, and Aaron has his permit. They can do all the driving," Mother replied. "You know Darcy and I have our Bible studies the nights the others go to the sports events."

"Please, Mom," Aaron pleaded.

Mother hugged Aaron. "Your mother will go," she said grinning at me, and I knew I was elected.

When we started out Thursday night for the game, Aaron informed us that we wouldn't have to pick up Madeleine that week. She was going to stay with friends and would meet us at the game.

As I entered the old familiar place where Tom and I had been together so many times, I was plunged into a feeling of deep sadness. But before I knew it, the game was over. As the crowd started to leave, Wanda and a friend came up to me. Wanda gave me a hug.

"You see, Mom, I told you it would be fun."

"It was," I admitted. "Now, let's beat the traffic." I still worried about the children driving; they seemed so young.

"Mother, could Aaron drive home?" Wanda asked. "I want to spend the night with Lillian."

I hesitated. "You know Aaron has only a permit. He is supposed to have a licensed driver with him at all times."

"Oh, Mom, who will know that you haven't got a license? Besides, tomorrow he gets his license."

"Let her go," Aaron said, having come near in time to hear most of the argument. I knew how happy he was to get behind the wheel. I finally relented, knowing that he drove just as well as Wanda.

We were almost through the outskirts of town and were headed toward home when the sudden blast of a police siren sounded right behind us. "Oh no," I groaned.

"Mom, I can't think of a thing I did wrong," Aaron said worriedly, as he pulled to the side of the road.

The surly deputy bounced up to the window and looked at Aaron suspiciously. "Let me see your driver's license," he barked.

Aaron handed him his permit. The officer looked at it.

"Well, I see you're out after curfew," he gloated.

"I—" Aaron started to explain, but the officer snapped, "Don't give me any backtalk, young man!" Then he turned his flashlight toward my face. "I bet you are too young to be out after curfew, also, young lady."

I'm sure my mouth flew open in surprise. Then I felt the laughter bubbling up inside me. "I think you just lost a bet, Officer." I giggled. "I happen to be this boy's mother!"

The deputy almost dropped his flashlight. He gave me a closer look, muttered something about women who never grew up, and said for us to go on home. He never even thought about asking to see the driver's license I didn't have.

Mother was waiting for us with cookies and hot chocolate, eager to hear all about our evening. She looked pleased when Aaron and I came in, talking and giggling like a couple of teenagers. "Sounds like you both had a good time," she said with a grin. "Did your team win?"

"We won, and Mom was the basketball queen in the stadium. All the men were giving her glances of admiration."

"Was Eric there?" Mother asked, a little frown forming above her glasses.

"He was there," Aaron said with a grin. "Miss La Salle, our new French teacher, cornered him the moment he walked in the door."

Mother looked thoughtful. "Is this Miss La Salle pretty?"

Aaron smiled. "She is quite a dish, if you like older women."

"How much older? And does Eric think she is, as you call it, 'quite a dish'? Whatever that means," she added quickly, squinting at him over the top of her glasses.

"Mother," I teased, "I believe you are jealous."

"I just don't want Eric to get hurt," Mother replied.

I knew what Mother wanted for Eric—me.

Aaron's voice cut into my thoughts. "Mom enjoyed the game and seeing friends again," he said, taking a swallow of the sweet hot drink. "But did you know that she isn't old enough to be out after curfew?"

Between gales of laughter we managed to tell Mother what had happened. She laughed until the tears slid down her face. I knew that she had already had a run-in or two with the new officer on her way to and from her weekly trips to the sale barn.

I'm sure that the officer was hoping he had seen the last of us, but it was not to be.

One evening just before bedtime, Mother heard on the radio that a bank robber had escaped from jail in the next county. He was thought to be headed our way. When we went to bed, Mother put the flashlight and Tom's old shotgun beside our bed. The gun once belonged to Tom's grandfather. We never did have any ammunition for it.

"A robber has no way of knowing that the gun isn't loaded," Mother said, leaning it against the night stand.

The wind had come up, and for hours I listened to the rattle and creaking of the old house. I must have dozed off when the squeaking of our old rocking chair in the living room woke me up with a start. Mother raised off her pillow at the same time. I opened my mouth to tell her about the creaking of the chair, but her hand stopped my words.

"Shhhhhhhh," she whispered, handing me the flashlight. "Don't turn it on until we reach the living room," she said softly. In the commotion I hadn't heard Wanda slip into the room, and I jumped when she hissed close to my other ear, "I've already called the police!"

About then, Aaron, who had recently discovered the freedom of sleeping in the nude, came sprinting down the hall. He reached our room before he remembered he was as naked as a singed chicken. Wildly, he groped around in the dark, searching for something with which to cover himself. We started our march down the hall, with Mother leading, holding the old gun. I was close on her heels with the flashlight. I could feel Aaron's breath warm on the back of my neck. Mother's long white nightgown floated eerily behind her. I crept as close to the ballooning gown as I could. Once, the old rocker gave an extra loud creak, and I jumped, stubbing my toe against Mother's bare heel.

Mother whispered, "Turn on the light," as she jerked open the door, yelling, "I'll blast any robber in this house to kingdom come!"

Forgetting my hurt toe, I pointed the light in the direction of the old rocking chair. There sat Kid, blinking in the sudden glare of the flashlight. The wind had blown open the door with the faulty catch, and Kid had come in seeking shelter from the storm.

At that moment, the same deputy who had stopped us on our way home from the game came into the room. I saw his eyes widen as his gaze riveted on Aaron. I turned to see why he was staring at the boy. It was then I wished there had been a robber in the house to take his attention away from my poor son.

There he stood, with Mother's old-fashioned corset, with its staves and laces hooked around his half-naked body.

After some explanations from us, the officer left, glaring suspiciously after the corseted Aaron and muttering, "This whole family belongs in a booby hatch!"

# Chapter 12

# Darcy's Essay

One afternoon I looked up from the pan of apples I was peeling to see Darcy skipping up the walk, followed by his teacher.

*Oh, no, not more school problems*, I thought, untying my apron and flinging it on the back of a chair before going to the door.

"Now what have you done?" I asked, as Darcy bounced up on the porch. He looked down at his scuffed boots but not before I saw the mischievous twinkle in his eyes and the elfin grin spread across his tanned face.

"Good afternoon, Mrs. Scra . . . ah . . . Gills," Lester Clark said, his voice husky with smothered laughter. "I do hope this is not a bad time to come calling. I remember you told me if I had any more of these to send home, I was to deliver them in person." He held a folded piece of paper out to me. I nodded, remembering our last encounter, and snatched the note out of his hand.

He gave me a moment to read it before adding, "You can see that Darcy's grades and deportment have very much improved. I'm proud of him, as I am sure you are."

Before I could answer, Mother bustled to the door with a big smile of welcome. "Come in, Mr. Clark," she insisted,

67

ushering us all to the kitchen table. "I just took oatmeal cookies out of the oven. Darcy tells me they are your favorite, Mr. Clark."

Now it was Lester Clark's turn to look somewhat embarrassed. I silently gloated as I watched him brush at a lock of reddish hair on his forehead before sitting down. Darcy was already helping himself to a hot cookie. The teacher laid a hand on his shoulder.

"Darcy has been very generous in sharing some of your excellent baking with me, Mrs. Lewis."

Mother looked pleased and passed the plate of warm cookies to him. "Come to dinner sometime, Mr. Clark, and I will prove I can cook something besides cookies."

Clark flashed me a quizzical look. "I'd like that, if Mrs. Gills has no objections."

"This is Mother's home, and she can invite to dinner whomever she wants," I said shortly.

Clark ignored my surly remark. "I really didn't come to entice a dinner invitation. I came to tell Mrs. Gills about the end-of-the-school-year program and Darcy's part in it. We have decided to combine our programs this year with the Sweetbrier rural school's. I guess I really came to invite you to attend the occasion with me, Mrs. Gills."

My heart raced. Each day my anger with life's problems softened. Still, I snapped into a defiant mood anytime a man singled me out for attention. Now, my mind groped for some excuse to refuse Lester Clark's invitation. I felt the silence close around me like a wall I was trying to see over. I heard Mother say, "Of course, Kate must go; she wouldn't want to disappoint Darcy."

"Mom, tell Mr. Clark you'll go with him," Darcy entreated so seriously that Clark looked amused.

"So far, it looks like everyone is on my side, Mrs. Gills. Will you make it unanimous?"

"Does 'unanimous' mean that Mom is coming with you, Mr. Clark?" Darcy asked quickly. "Well, does it, Mom?" Darcy's questioning eyes were big with excitement.

"I guess so," I said, and everyone looked at me as if I

had just said something very profound.

"It's Monday afternoon, Mom," Darcy said, breaking the silence. "That's the last day of school before summer vacation."

Mr. Clark stood up. "I'll call for you about one-thirty, Mrs. Gills," he said quickly. He seemed in a rush to get away before I changed my mind.

"Thanks for the cookies, Mrs. Lewis," he said over his shoulder as he went out the door.

I laughed as I watched him scurry down the path.

"Your cookies really sent him off at a lope, Gram."

She gave me a hug as we turned from the door.

"I think it was the surprise of your accepting his invitation that put wings on his heels," she said and giggled.

"Mr. Clark is always in a hurry," Darcy added. "He says we all have so many things to accomplish in life; and time is so precious, we should never waste it."

"You like Mr. Clark, don't you?" Gram said, studying his serious, upturned face.

"Yup," he said, going to the table for another cookie. "We are friends. I'm glad you are going with us, Mom."

I asked, "Will you be going with Mr. Clark too?"

Darcy frowned. "I can't walk all the way to the Sweetbrier schoolhouse."

"That's fine, Darcy," I said, suddenly relieved of the anxieties of riding alone with Mr. Clark.

When the teacher arrived the next day with three other students in the car, I felt almost jubilant.

The schoolroom was already a bustle of activity when we got there. Lester found a spot with two empty chairs in the back of the crowded room. "Save one for me," he said as he smiled and excused himself. I saw him assembling his students in the front of the room, where seats were reserved for those taking part in the program. He had just returned to the seat beside me, when the Sweetbrier teacher stepped to the front of the room. After a brief introduction, she announced that Darcy Gills was to open the program with his original essay on deportment.

Darcy looked out over the crowd and turned pale. For an instant I thought he was going to turn and run! Then his eyes met mine. A wide grin spread across his face, and he lifted the paper in his hand and started to read.

"After my daddy died, I hurt all the time in my heart. At first I was angry with God for taking him away, but I went right on reading my Bible stories. The stories kept telling me to love everybody. They helped me to love the kids at school who did and said mean things to me. Now they are my friends, and my heart doesn't hurt like it used to. . . ."

When Darcy finished, there were few dry eyes in the room. Darcy waved his paper at me, and I heard the applause as he received a standing ovation.

"I'm proud to have had a small part in this," Clark said, turning to look at me. "Darcy is a very special little boy!"

I was still groping for a tissue to wipe my eyes when he offered his own handkerchief. "I am sure that you had a big part in helping Darcy cope with the problems his father's death brought on," I replied.

Eric was in the kitchen having hot chocolate and talking with Mother when we returned. He stood up and pulled back a chair for me at the table. Darcy shoved his own chair as close as he could to Eric's.

"Eric," he said with eyes shining, "people clapped their hands and then stood up and clapped some more when I read my essay."

Eric put his hand on Darcy's shoulder. "Sorry I wasn't there to join all those people applauding you, Big Shot. I know your mother is very proud of you."

Darcy shrugged. "She cried. Mr. Clark had to wipe her tears away with his handkerchief."

I felt my face turn pink as Eric looked at me. For an instant his eyes studied my face as if searching for some hidden clue. Then, with a slight grin, he said, "Your mother is always losing her handkerchief."

"Is that why you got her all those fancy ones for Christmas?" Darcy asked, and the uncomfortable moment was broken as we all laughed at the serious look on Darcy's face.

"That must have been my reason," Eric said, rubbing his hand over Darcy's stubble of hair that had been barbered by his gram that morning for the school event. "Now that school is out, what are your plans for the summer?"

Darcy's eyes danced with excitement. "I got a job. I'm going to milk Miss Bell's goat and read my Bible stories to her too. I don't get money for reading the Bible stories. Mom said God's words are free for everybody to hear."

"Miss Bell will probably pay you well for milking her goat. You'll be well off when summer is over."

Darcy looked serious. "Gram said if I save part of my money whenever I work and put it in the bank, she will add to it. That way, by the time I graduate from the country school, I can go to the academy. I want to go to a school where I'll learn more about God."

Eric looked pleased. "Saving for something *that* important shows good sense. I hope you'll let me add a little to that bank account too. I like to help those who are working to make our world a better place for us all."

"Will my learning about God make the world better?"

"Sure it will, if you share what you learn with others."

"I will," Darcy said, his face solemn. "I'll shout it from the housetop."

Mother hugged him and giggled. "We had better leave the rooftop for Kid to play on. I think more people would hear you if you had your own little church."

Darcy's eyes reflected his excitement. "Could I really have a church?"

"No reason why not, if you are willing to plow a straight furrow to help the Lord."

## Chapter 13

# Closing Another Chapter

My eyes were riveted on Wanda, who sat in the front row of graduates on the stage.

Today, my daughter is closing another chapter of her life and mine, I thought.

I was so involved in watching my little Wanda that I was surprised to hear Eric's voice.

"She is beautiful," he whispered.

I smiled at Eric and glanced at Mother's happy up-turned face, beaming with pride as she watched her granddaughter crossing the stage to receive her diploma. She must have felt my gaze, for she turned her head and looked at me. I saw the tears that glistened on her lashes.

"Thanks, Mother," I whispered, "for helping us make this day possible."

She gave me one of her old mischievous grins. "We have all been plowing a straight furrow," she said softly, giving my arm a squeeze.

As we were leaving the auditorium, I saw a pretty young woman in a beautifully tailored blue suit and yellow blouse moving like a gazelle toward Eric. I felt my backbone stiffen, as I waited for Eric to make the introductions.

Her name was Cherrie La Salle. She had a firm handshake and eyes that were penetrating and assured. Not being able to find a single flaw with her pretty features added to my feeling of frustration. I knew she had to have brains to be a teacher. *Well, good for you, Eric,* I thought, but for some reason I wasn't feeling any sincere good wishes for their continuing friendship. I was suddenly uncomfortably aware of my old gray suit and the pink blouse that had seen too many washings.

I felt stiff and matronly as I watched Miss La Salle glide away in her stylish high-heeled shoes, tapping a tattoo on the hardwood floor.

Aaron gave me a look. "See what I was talking about, Mom? Didn't I describe her pretty well?"

I felt my face burn and jabbed Aaron in the ribs with my elbow, hoping Eric was too busy watching the departure of Miss La Salle to have heard his remark. Eric turned and looked at Aaron.

"Don't you and Miss La Salle get along? I've heard she is rather strict with her pupils."

"I'm not one of her students," Aaron said. "I won't take a foreign language class until next year. I was just telling Mom the other night how pretty Miss La Salle is."

Eric looked at me with a mischievous twinkle in his blue eyes. "Not as pretty as your mother, when she minds her manners."

I made a face at him. "It is going to take more than you and Mother to improve my behavior." I chuckled, locking arms through theirs and walking toward the door.

Wanda had only been away at school about three months when her letters started to mention a young man she had met. He was attending barber college not far from the beauty school.

Mother laughed one day when I read aloud Wanda's latest letter filled with glowing accounts of the young man whose name was William Largent. "Sounds like our other man-hater has met her match at last," Mother said. "Only months ago she told us she would rather kiss a horse than a boy and that she was sure she would never see a boy through the eyes of love."

"When this young man starts to act like a suitor instead of a friend, Wanda may again change her tune," I replied.

"Not if he is the right one," Mother said wisely. Mother was right, as usual. When Wanda came home for the holidays at Christmas, she was wearing an engagement ring. It seemed that her every other word was something about this wonderful man she planned to marry when they finished their training.

"William has already been promised a job in the barbershop next door to Aunt Olive's beauty shop," Wanda said. "Isn't that wonderful, since I'll be working for Auntie?"

"I'm afraid this is all happening too fast," I said, worry making my voice sound stern.

"Mother, it was you and Gram who encouraged me to be nice to the opposite sex. Now that I've found a man I really like, you are acting as though I'm doing something wrong."

I tried to calm her. "I know you aren't doing anything wrong, Honey. It's just that we don't know anything about this young man."

"William wanted to come home with me to meet you, but his mother just had surgery. He thought she needed him at home this Christmas.

"Mom, you and Gram will meet him and his mother when we get married in the spring. William has promised we will have the wedding right here in our little church. I knew you would want that, Mother. Please say you are happy for me."

"Of course I am, Honey. I guess I'll just have to trust your good sense and fine judgment of character. You know I want only the best for you."

"Don't worry, Mom. You will love William." She giggled. "So will you, Gram. William plows a straight furrow too."

Mother laughed. "Are you sure now that you like him better than your horse?"

Wanda grinned. "I'm sure, Gram."

## Chapter 14

# Mothers-in-Law!

Wanda kept up a steady stream of chatter as I sat on the floor to pin the hem of her wedding dress. I was hearing only half of what she was saying, until she announced, "Mom, I told William's mother she could spend the night here with you after the wedding."

"You what?" I gasped, almost swallowing a mouthful of pins.

"I thought it would be nice for both of you," Wanda said, looking a little wistful. "You will like William's mother. You both have so much in common."

I laughed. "How can we have anything in common? You told me William's mother is a successful businesswoman. I'm only an old-lady farmer."

She gave me a little shake. "Now, you just stop putting yourself down, Mom," she said sternly.

"You are a good daughter," I said, helping her get the dress off over her blonde curls, but my mind raced with the thoughts of the intimidating house guest.

The old farm house wasn't the place to invite a career woman from the big city to stay overnight. She would have to sleep in Wanda's old room. It hadn't been painted in years. The rug was worn thin from years of hard-soled shoes scuffing across it.

That wasn't the only worry. What would I have to talk about with this woman? We lived in different worlds.

The next two days I sewed and worried. Would William's mother be as uncomfortable trying to be gracious in the awkward situation our children were putting us in?

The day of the wedding arrived bright and sunny. Happy is the bride the sun shines on, I thought, as I trudged to the barn to do chores. It seemed only yesterday that this bride-to-be was running ahead of me to open the barn door, eager to feed a calf or curry a pony.

Just before noon I heard Wanda shout, "They're here!"

I looked out to see a tall young man and a smartly-dressed woman coming up the walk. Wanda had flung open the door and was pulling me toward it.

"Mom," she said with pride, "this is William—"

Wanda's words were lost, as the woman at his side gave a small cry, "*Kate Lewis*—is that really *you?*"

"Grace," I gasped, and rushed to hug her while our children stared in disbelief.

Grace and I spent the rest of the day reminiscing. We had been best friends all through grammar school in Idaho. Both our families were working class and had seen some hard times. As kids we learned to make the best with what we had.

I no longer worried about the condition of Wanda's old room. My sister Olive and I had often slept sardine-style with Grace and her sister Peggy in a double bed, either at her house or mine.

One time the four of us were out in the woods picking wild blackberries. I had scratched my arm on a bramble. When I went to pour some berries into Grace's bucket, the scratch bled on the sleeve of her white blouse. I felt terrible about the stain, but Grace had only laughed.

"Now our friendship is sealed in blood," she said.

It was shortly after this that Grace moved with her parents to Montana. At first our letters had passed back and forth each week. Then, as we both got involved with other friends, the letters tapered off and finally stopped.

I hadn't thought of my old friend in years. Now, as we talked, it was as if the twenty years apart had never existed.

That evening, we sat together in the small church while our children were married. When the minister pronounced them man and wife, I stole a look at my friend's face. I saw a tear roll down her smooth cheek.

I reached over and took her hand. "They gave us back the friendship we lost in the shuffle of life," I said softly. Grace brushed at the tears on her cheek and gripped my hand a little tighter. Than she grinned. "This time, instead of blood, it's sealed in love," she whispered.

"I'm glad our kids found each other and made us more than friends," I said.

Grace grinned, "Yeah, *Mothers-in-law!*"

Mother looked at us, a twinkle in her eyes.

"Someday, God willing, grandmothers!"

Grace's eyebrows shot up. "I never thought of that."

Mother hugged us and said, "You'll like being grandmothers."

Grace looked at me and shrugged. "At least we're in this together."

"Sealed with love," I said.

## Chapter 15

# Reaching for God's Hand

I wrote, "Dear Aaron," then sat with pen poised above the writing paper. He had been in the army almost a year and still each time I started a letter my heart pounded as it had the day he told me he was going to enlist.

"Why do you want to go?" I had demanded, as pictures of the war raging in Korea and the brother I had lost in World War II flashed before my eyes.

"Mother, you know I'm old enough for the draft. They could call me any time."

"They might not" I had insisted. "We have a farm; men are deferred if they are needed at home."

"I want to get it over with," Aaron had said stubbornly. I had just set the pen to paper again when a knock on the door made me jump. Probably Eric, come to see if Darcy and I needed transportation while Mother was visiting Olive.

I opened the door and stood speechless, afraid to believe my eyes.

"Aren't you even going to say Hello?" the dear familiar voice asked, and Aaron was holding me in a bear hug.

I brushed at my tears and looked at the handsome boy in uniform, duffel bag in hand, asking me, "What's for supper?" as if he had just returned from his evening chores.

"How did you get here? Why didn't you let me know you were coming?" My words came tumbling out, not waiting for answers.

"Didn't know it myself until three days ago—been traveling ever since. Got a lift on a plane but had to go the long way around to use it."

"You didn't tell me you expected a furlough any time soon."

He looked a little nervous. "It's not exactly a furlough."

"You're not in any trouble?" I asked, fear clutching at my heart.

"No," he said, and shot me a look of tender understanding. "I'm going overseas."

"Oh, no," I gasped. "You were in school taking some kind of training. Something to do with radar, you said in your last letter. I am so proud of you."

"I was, but I asked for overseas duty," he said, avoiding my eyes.

"Whatever for?" I cried, angry with him now. How could he do this? He knew what his going overseas would mean to me.

Aaron looked at me, and his eyes pleaded for understanding. "It was the only way I could get home to marry Madeleine. I was lucky, Mom. They are sending me to Alaska, not Korea."

I looked at him as if seeing him for the first time. This thin, serious-faced stranger. He will look like this when he is very old. Strong, wise, and a little stern. I sat down at the table, and he sat across from me. I thought of all the girls who had married the soldiers leaving for overseas in that other war. So many of those marriages had ended in divorce when the boys returned. The young men changed from the horror of war, or the girls found someone else while their husbands were away.

"I suppose Madeleine is all in accord with your marriage plans," I said, trying to keep the resentment out of my voice, but he knew me too well.

"Don't blame Madeleine," he said sharply. "She doesn't know about my plans."

"Then what makes you so sure she will go along with this crazy idea?" I asked, new hope soaring up inside me.

"You know that Madeleine and I have always planned to get married someday."

Yes, I knew. I had even hoped that Madeleine, the little tomboy who had followed my son around since grade school, would someday be his wife. But in the far, far future. Why, they were only babies. Aaron couldn't even get married without my consent. The thought warmed me, and for an instant, I hugged it close. I didn't have to give my consent.

Aaron was watching me anxiously. "Mom you wouldn't stop us?"

"We will talk this over with your grandma," I said, hedging for time. "She will be home tomorrow from her visit with Olive. We have to consider this very carefully."

"What's to consider?" he asked impatiently. "I just want to marry the girl I love."

"It's a big step you are asking me to let you take, Honey. You are so young—only a boy."

Aaron sniffed. "Uncle Sam doesn't seem to think I'm only a kid!" He stood up. "I'd better go see if Madeleine agrees with him."

I watched him go out the door, his back straight with defiance. As I climbed the stairs to his room, I was thankful my mother would be returning in the morning. I needed someone to talk to. Then I thought how close Aaron and his grandmother had always been and wondered if she would be my ally.

Aaron's room was just as he had left it when he went away. I hadn't been able to change a thing. Not even the sheets on his bed. Now, as I pulled them off, there was a soft thud as something hit the floor. I recognized at once the small flat rock. Aaron had found it on one of our many walks together. He was nine at the time; there had been something about the size and shape of the rock that held his fancy. It had become his talisman. When he went to bed unhappy, I would find him sleeping with the small rock clutched tightly in his small, grubby hand. He must have held it so that last night at home. With a lump in my throat, I placed it on the night stand beside the bed.

I was in the kitchen preparing Aaron's favorite breakfast when he came downstairs the next morning. He was wearing the old jeans that had been too short when he left, and now there was even a longer space between ankle and jeans.

"Boy, something besides army chow," he said, sitting down and leaning his elbows on the table. *A habit the army hasn't improved*, I thought with a grin, as I poured him a cup of hot chocolate.

"You aren't going to wear *those* clothes all day, are you?"

He pretended surprised. "What's wrong with them?" He brushed at the sleeve of the old sweat shirt.

"They were worn out before you went away. Besides, you have outgrown them."

Aaron looked down at the gap between sock and pants and grinned. "They are a little short," he said, extending his leg and making them look even shorter.

"I want you to put on your uniform before your grandma gets home."

His eyes lighted up. "I know Gram will understand my wanting to get married."

I turned back to the stove. Why couldn't I just say, "I understand, but I can't agree with you." I arranged the eggs on his plate and put it on the table.

"What did Madeleine think of your sudden idea to get married?"

"Oh, she agrees; we both know that life is very unsure these days. Whatever time we have we want to spend together."

"I'll bet her mother doesn't feel the same way."

Aaron frowned. "Not exactly, but Madeleine is of age. She will marry me with or without her mother's consent." A frown creased his brow. "It's not fair that a girl is of age at eighteen, but a boy who is old enough to go to war has to ask his mother if he can get married!" His voice was high and angry.

"I guess I'm the only fly in the ointment," I said, trying to sound flippant, but my voice trembled, and I felt the sting of tears behind my eyelids.

"I'm afraid so, Mom." His eyes pleaded with me until I had to look away.

We ate in silence. The idea of the marriage stood between us like a stark and ugly wall. The food stuck to my throat, and I might as well have dumped dry cereal from a box for all the attention Aaron was giving his favorite buttermilk pancakes. He ate hurriedly and then excused himself. I felt the anger in his heavy stomp upon the stairs as he went to his room. What in the world was I going to do? Tell him to go ahead and ruin his life? No matter what I did now, I had lost him.

Aaron came back to the kitchen dressed in his uniform; he looked at me defiantly. "Well, your little boy has obeyed," he said sullenly.

I felt my face crumple and covered it with my hands as my shoulders shook with sobs. Aaron was at my side immediately with his arm around my shoulder, dabbing at my eyes with his handkerchief. "Oh, Mom, I was only ribbing you."

I took the handkerchief and scrubbed at my eyes. "What are you going to do until lunch time?"

"You said Gram was coming home."

"She probably won't get here before noon. You could spend the morning with Madeleine."

"Thanks, Mom," he said quickly, and after giving me a brief hug, went out the door.

I stood at the window and watched as he walked down the lane. Again the sumac bushes were flaming red, and behind them the tall oaks shimmered like gold. It was just such a day when I had seen him off for his first day of school. In my mind I saw him turn and wave a small brown hand. . . .

When my mother arrived, she took one look at me and asked, "Honey, are you ill?"

As quickly as I could, I told her of Aaron's arrival and his determination to get married. Mother listened until I stopped for breath.

"What's so terrible about Aaron's getting married?" Mother asked, pouring herself a cup of hot chocolate and sitting down at the table across from me.

"You know what's so terrible," I wailed. "He is still a boy—barely nineteen years old."

"A year older than you were when you got married," Mother said, pursing her lips as was her habit when reflecting on something.

"You didn't like it either, did you?" I accused.

"At the time I suppose I felt very much like you are feeling now. But were you ever sorry?"

"Oh, no," I said quickly. "We had so little time as things turned out. Still, our getting married right after Tom got out of high school didn't give him any time to prepare for the future. I want so much more for Aaron than his father and I had."

Mother shrugged. "Is it fair that you think of Aaron's life as an extension of yours? He is an individual with longings and desires of his own."

"*Aaron is all I have*," I said stubbornly, not thinking about Darcy, and went upstairs to make the beds.

Again I found the rock under Aaron's pillow. Picking it up, I sat on the edge of the bed. *Dear God, help me to handle this*, I prayed, trying to swallow the lump in my throat. I closed my eyes and saw a little boy with tear-tangled lashes holding the stone in a small grubby hand. When I had asked Aaron why he held the rock, he had replied: "Mom, I hold the rock when I reach out for God's hand."

Last night, Aaron's hand, no longer small, had held the talisman with a heavy heart, and it was my fault.

"Oh, Darling," I sobbed. "I only want your happiness." I wiped my tears from the stone and slipped it into my apron pocket.

At lunch time Aaron turned his attention to his beloved grandmother. I listened with racing pulse while he told what he had done to get home. "I had to put in for overseas duty. I knew it was my only chance of getting back to marry Madeleine. I prayed every night for my orders to come through. When they finally did, I whooped with joy, and the guys thought I was crazy."

"You must really want to get married to have gone to such desperate lengths to get home," Gram said.

"More than anything in the world," Aaron replied, looking straight at me. My heart raced, and I touched the small rock in my apron pocket.

"Well," I said, "it's not as if I'm losing a son; I'll be gaining a daughter."

Aaron nearly knocked the table over trying to get to my side. "What made you change your mind?" he whispered, while giving me a hug.

"This," I said, handing him the rock. He grinned and slipped it into his pocket.

It was a small wedding at Madeleine's home. I have never seen a happier couple stand before a minister. When the pastor asked us to spend a moment of silent prayer, I bowed my head, but my mind raced. *Gone forever is the small wistful boy who looked to me for comfort.*

The prayer was over, and I raised my head as Aaron turned to his bride. His look of reverence and Madeleine's answering smile were like a halo of love around them. I felt the tears on my cheeks. I groped in my purse for a handkerchief and smiled as my hand closed around Aaron's talisman.

*Son, I'll remember to reach out for God's hand,* I said silently, as I wiped away my tears.

# Chapter 16

# Attack!

One afternoon I decided to check the fence between our place and Mike Marshal's. I didn't want any more trouble with that obnoxious man.

I found a slack span in the fence and was stretching it for stapling when I heard a sound behind me. I turned but could see nothing moving near the trees. I took another staple from my pocket and raised the hammer. There were footsteps behind me. I swung around and froze with dread. There stood Mike Marshal. He must have been hiding behind a tree. He had advanced so close, I could smell the liquor on his breath. I remembered the day I had gone with him to get the horses out of his field. My heart raced with apprehension.

"What are you doing here?" I asked, trying to appear calm.

"You don't seem very happy to see me, Katie. I came to help you."

"I don't need your help. How did you know I was here?"

"Are you forgetting it's my land on the other side of the fence?" he smirked.

"Then why are you on *my* side of it?" I shot back at him.

"You will know soon enough, Katie, my dear."

"I'm not your *dear*, and I don't like you calling me that!" I said testily.

Marshal took another step in my direction. "I don't like you being so unfriendly either."

"Let's face it, Marshal; we don't like each other. I've got no time to argue with you!" I started to walk away, but he caught my arm. Terror made me tremble. I was a scrapper, but I knew I was no match for his strength. I was miles from the nearest house.

"You can't hold me here!"

"I can keep you long enough." There was a tinge of red in his eyes.

He was laughing at me now. "I set my sights on you a long time ago; nothing can stop me now."

I managed to wrench my arm free and started to run. He sprang in front of me. I raised the hammer, and let the blow fall on his shoulder. This only enraged him. I raised the hammer again. He grabbed my arm, and I felt the twisting of my wrist. I cried out in pain.

I heard Eric's voice, loud with anger. I thought I was imagining it until I felt the hand release my wrist and saw Eric with Marshal wrapped around his neck like a scarf. Eric spun, and I saw Marshal fly over the fence. I heard him grunt as he landed on his stomach in his own field.

Eric turned to me. "Kate, are you all right?" he asked tenderly, eyes filled with worry.

"I think my wrist is broken," I said, but I was still looking at Marshal. "Is he hurt?"

Eric glanced at Marshal with scorn. "Can't hurt a drunk."

Marshal lifted his head and ducked it again when he saw Eric looking at him.

"You need help, Marshal?" Eric asked, his voice as cold as steel.

Marshal quietly got to his feet and stumbled off across the field.

"I'll take care of him later," Eric said. "Now let's get you home."

I was suddenly conscious of my ripped blouse. I tried to

pull it over my bare shoulder and winced with pain.

Eric pulled my blouse together, his eyes stern with anger.

"At least your wrist isn't broken, or you couldn't have pulled your blouse over your shoulder." He lifted my arm tenderly and inspected it. "Starting to swell; better get you home and put some cold compresses on this." He picked me up and started to walk toward his horse, which was in the shade of a tree.

For a moment I relaxed in the comfort of the strong, safe arms around me. The feeling of pleasure and languor was new and disconcerting. I stiffened and tried to free myself. "I can walk," I said shortly. "Only my wrist is hurt."

Eric only grinned at me. "I know you can walk, Kate. but I don't think you can get on the horse with that wrist." He set me behind the saddle. "Sorry you have to ride back there," he said, swinging astride. "You couldn't control 'Old Hard Mouth' with the reins in your left hand."

"How did you know where I was today?" I asked.

"Your mother thought you might need some help repairing the fence."

"Thank God for my mother and for a good friend like you," I said, and tightened my arm around his waist.

Darcy slid off his burro as we rode into the yard.

"What happened?" he asked, his eyes expressing sudden worry. "Why is Mom riding on your horse? Gram said she was repairing the fence."

Eric put a hand on Darcy's shoulder. "Your mother sprained her wrist. Where is your grandmother?"

"Gram went to the sale."

"I'm surprised you didn't go with her," I said, knowing how he loved the excitement of the sale barn.

I winced as Eric lifted me off the horse and my hand brushed against his arm.

"I wanted to go with Gram," Darcy said, "but Miss Bell has some work for me. I'd better get over there." He climbed on the burro; then he turned a worried look my way.

"Do you need me, Mom?"

"No, Honey, I'm fine; I only have a little sprain." Darcy waved his storybook at us and was off in a cloud of dust.

"My last little bird is growing up fast," I said, watching him disappear around the bend in the lane. My eyes were suddenly moist.

Eric, sensitive to my moods, placed his arm around my shoulder. "Kate, there will always be some feeling of sadness as our lives change. It's all part of living."

His arm around my shoulder was comforting. It brought out the usual companionable feelings I took for granted when he was around and missed when he was away. I glanced up at him and felt my face turn pink. What was I reading in that gentle look I hadn't seen before? For a brief moment I felt the tension in his body before he took his arm away.

"We had better get some cold compresses on your wrist," he said briskly. He started to walk away, then turned and looked at me. "Kate, I think it's time we had a talk." For a second his eyes looked deep into mine; then he went to the sink and started the water running into a basin. I was trembling. Must be the shock from my ordeal this afternoon, I told myself. But it was no use pretending; I knew what Eric was going to say.

Eric was in the process of wrapping a cold cloth around my wrist. "Kate, I think you know what I am going to ask you," he said solemnly. "We have been friends too long to be able to hide our feelings from each other."

"Sure I know what you're going to ask me. I'm a mind reader," I said, groping for a touch of my old banter while stalling for time. Eric sat in a chair beside me. He looked down at his hands that were so tightly locked together, the knuckles showed white.

"Kate, you know I loved Tom like a brother. And the day I met his wife, I loved her too. I vowed I'd find a girl just like her to marry."

"Why didn't you find that girl?" I asked, my breath coming fast.

"I was still looking when Tom died. His death put me in an awkward position. Now there was only you, and my loving you didn't seem quite right. I fought my feelings for you, Kate. I grew up with a mother as devout as yours. I knew it was wrong to covet another man's wife, so I tried even harder to find one of my own."

I thought of the lovely Miss La Salle. "You never lacked for women friends," I said testily.

Eric grinned. "I hoped you would notice that I was trying."

I felt a new tenderness toward him. I hadn't known he felt like this. "Eric, there are many different kinds of love. First love is often just the bloom of youth."

"I know what I felt when I saw you go off with that doctor. Then there was Darcy's teacher."

I grinned at him. "Why, Eric Johnson, I do believe you were jealous," I teased.

"It was then I started to ask myself the question."

"What question, Eric?"

He looked at me thoughtfully. "Would I want my best friend to have my most cherished possession if I died?"

"And what was your answer to that question?"

He shrugged. "I didn't like the answer."

"Will you tell me what it was?"

Eric sighed. "Kate, if my dearest possession were you, I would want more for you than the fate of a farmer's wife. When I noticed your going out with a doctor and a teacher, I knew I would have to give you a chance to find someone who could give you and the children more than I would ever be able to."

Again I felt the tears blurring my vision. I slipped my hand into his. "Eric, sometimes you are as kind and compassionate as my little Darcy. I'm surprised you didn't become a minister."

There was a glint of mischief in his blue eyes. "Kate, I don't think any woman would let me keep you as my best friend. Will you marry me?"

I grinned at him. "I'll have to write and tell Aaron that

the man I'm going to marry isn't smaller than he is, but he is willing to get the wood and milk the cows."

Eric chuckled. "I think the children will accept me," he said, taking me in his arms.

"Don't forget Mother," I said softly, snuggling close as the happiness that had eluded me for so long swept over me.

"Your mother always knew this was going to happen. I heard her drive into the yard. Let's go tell her the news!"

I held back. "Only the good news," I said, looking at my arm. "Let everyone think I got this while repairing the fence."

Eric shrugged. "All I can say is, Marshal is lucky I won't do anything to give the neighbors cause to gossip about you."

"Thanks," I whispered, as Mother bustled into the kitchen.

"Well, what are you two whispering about?" she asked, looking at us closely. "You both look like bluebirds of happiness."

Eric gave her a hug. "That describes how I'm feeling since I just learned that you are going to be my mother-in-law."

Happiness danced in Mother's eyes. "I thought you would never ask," she giggled. "Now Darcy and I can hold down the old homestead. With my son-in-law's help, of course."

"Mother, there will always be room in my house for both you and Darcy."

"I know that, Son," she said with a grin. "But newlyweds need time to spend alone. Darcy and I will be happy here after you take this feisty daughter off my hands."

It was then she saw the bandage on my arm. "I see she got another hurt today trying to do a man's work."

Eric looked stern. "I'll take good care of her, Mother. You just hurry with the wedding plans."

## Chapter 17

# The Return of Sunshine

It was a small but beautiful wedding. The church was decorated with flowers and filled with family and close friends. As I looked out over the sea of happy, upturned faces, my heart soared with joy. I could feel the love and best wishes around me like a warm cloak. A feeling of peace came over me. I glanced at Eric and knew this marriage was right. I would put it in God's hands where it would be safe.

My sister Olive was my matron of honor, and her husband Edward was Eric's best man. Despite how perfect everything seemed, Eric and I were as nervous as a teenage couple on their wedding day.

Instead of a honeymoon, we went directly to Eric's large old farmhouse. We were rural folks and knew this was not the time of year to be away from the farm.

My life with Eric was filled with happiness and peace of mind. The feelings of guilt and betrayal I'd expected when I married again did not materialize.

Eric and I were both as busy as before, but we found time for quiet talks and companionship. Often we walked hand in hand like young lovers in the woods while looking for a stray calf or lamb. We spent quiet evenings sitting on the back porch of the old house Eric's father had built for his bride years before our time. Here, we listened to the sleepy call of a restless bird and watched the moon rise above the treetops. I never knew these simple pleasures could mean so much when shared with someone so in accord with my own feelings.

I was learning that marriage can go beyond the physical to become almost spiritual in nature. Yes, at last I had put my hand on the proverbial plow and had stopped looking back.

Mother watched the change in me and was filled with pride and happiness. One day, when I was spending the afternoon with her, she said with a saucy grin, "You are plowing a straight furrow, Partner. I knew you could do it, Honey; I've never raised a failure yet."

Eric and I gave the Christmas dinner that year. Wanda and William and Olive and Edward came down together the night before.

Christmas morning, my dear friend Grace arrived to spend the holidays with us. This not only made me especially happy, but also made her son William's day complete. He was very anxious to tell us some good news. He waited until we were gathered around the table before he told us.

Wanda, all smiles, tapped her water glass with her spoon and with a fond glance at her husband, said, "Everyone better listen to William's announcement before he bursts trying to hold it back."

William blushed and for a minute seemed tongue-tied. Then he gave Gram a roguish grin. "Gram, it was your idea for Wanda and me to turn our two moms into grandmothers."

Mother looked at him over her glasses. "I forgot to tell you, but that will really make me GREAT!"

We all laughed and started talking about plans for the little stranger's arrival. It was a perfect day, bountiful with love and caring. Aaron and Madeleine's absence was the only sadness the day held. It was tempered, however, by the knowledge that Madeleine had been able to join Aaron in Alaska just before Christmas. They would be alone, but I felt sure they knew they were with us in thought and in all our prayers. I remembered how happy Aaron's letters had become since his marriage. I was relieved to know I had not spoiled that love they so wanted to share. I silently thanked God for the courage to let go of the ties that can become too binding.

That winter I felt my life had never been more fulfilled or tranquil. These were days of joy and sunshine. The happy scenes of three children growing up with their zany farm animals danced in my memory each time I stood at the kitchen window and reflected on what had turned out to be a rich and wonderful life.

I was thrilled at the prospect of a baby in our family again. Mother and I spent many happy hours together reminiscing as I sewed baby clothes and she knitted on a sweater with matching booties. It was almost like the times we had shared while waiting for our little Wanda to arrive. Now Wanda was going to have a little one of her own. Where had all the years gone so quickly? we asked each other, as we sewed and remembered all the love and happiness we had shared. So many blessings.

We never knew that winter, as we dreamed and planned, how soon these happy days would end. There was no warning that tragedy would soon strike our family again. . . .

# Chapter 18

# A Red Star for Mother

Mother never realized her dream of holding her first great-grandchild in her arms. She was not as tough as her old barrel cactus. It was still sitting prickly and sturdy on the window-sill that early morning when we rushed her to the hospital for gallstone surgery.

Mother suffered terribly after her surgery. Everything seemed to go wrong at once.

On the tenth day, the doctor asked me to wait in the small room at the end of the corridor while he examined Mother. After what seemed ages to me, the doctor came in to talk to me. I looked at him mutely, too filled with fear to ask any of the questions haunting me.

"Your mother has a lot of problems," he said kindly. "The kidneys have almost stopped functioning. There is some internal bleeding, and her heart is growing steadily weaker."

The doctor was paged, and I went back to Mother's room. I sat as close to the bed as I could get. Her face was so white and drawn. Her eyes were open, but she didn't seem to see or hear the things around her. Each breath she drew was a moan of pain.

Eric stayed with me as long as he could and promised to return with Darcy after the evening chores. We both

94

knew the end was near. Eric had just left when Mother raised her head off the pillow. For a second, her eyes lighted up.

"Take me now, dear Lord," she whispered.

Fear gripped me. "You are going to be all right," I said softly, taking her hand in mine. "You are tough like your old cactus, remember?"

"No," she said, "that is all over now."

Suddenly, her pain-drawn face was radiantly beautiful, and the smile that touched her lips was angelic. I stood up and leaned over to kiss her. "I love you," I whispered.

For a second she snuggled in my arms like a small child; then she closed her eyes, and I knew she was gone.

The nurse came in, and I walked to the small room at the end of the corridor. She was gone, the one person in all the world who I had taken for granted would always be there when I needed her.

When Eric arrived to take me home, he was alone.

"Darcy was still at Miss Bell's when I got your call. I thought it best to tell him later," he said, putting his arm around my shoulder.

"Thanks for understanding," I said softly. "We both know how hard this is going to be for him."

"It's not going to be easy for you," he said, kissing my cheek. "Shall we go together to tell him now?"

I shook my head. "Eric, will you please drop me off at Mother's house while you go pick up Darcy? I need to be alone for just a little while."

A worried frown furrowed his brow. "Are you sure you want to be alone? I could come with you."

"Please, Eric, I need this quiet time with God."

I stood on the porch until Eric drove out of the yard before I opened the kitchen door and stepped inside.

Everything looked just the same. The sunlight shimmered across the old oak table. It had always been one of the favorite spots in the room.

Today, the table held only Mother's well-worn Bible and a brand new book of Bible stories. Seeing the new book brought a gentle smile to my lips. Mother had been spoiling Darcy again with yet another coveted book.

On the other side of the old cookstove was Mother's favorite chair, where she so often sat with Darcy at her knee while they studied the Bible or solved a problem.

The rocker could tell so many stories, if it could talk. One my mother often told was about how she was once a total prisoner in the old chair.

On that particular day, she had been rocking my sister Olive to sleep. I had slipped around behind the chair and tied Mother to it by her apron strings. She couldn't get loose until Father came home hours later and untied her. I had tied the knots, but I couldn't untie them.

I walked over to the window where Mother had placed her cactus. A cry of awe escaped my lips when I saw that the cactus was crowned with a soft cloud of beauty. Five large, bell-shaped blossoms stood upon that homely, prickly pedestal.

"Oh, Mother," I said aloud, "your ugly cactus does have a time of beauty."

As I stood there, admiring the plant with feelings of wonder and reverence, I remembered Mother's angelic smile. My tears rolled down freely. In that moment, I felt sure Mother had known that everything the Lord creates has a time of beauty. I walked over to where the blackboard hung on the wall. In Mother's neat handwriting were the words:

> Silly Biddy. . . . . Sep. 10
> Golden Bell. . . . .Feb. 24
> Red Lady. . . . . . Mar. 2

Below this were the family names and the red stars they had earned.

I picked up the chalk and wrote Mother's name, making a large red star at the end of it.

"For you, Mother," I whispered. "You are the one who really earned the red star. It was you who showed us all how to plow a straight furrow."